Praise

The Jetlaunch customer support is lightning fast, and the quality of their work is ON FIRE. They finished my project much faster than I expected. Use Jetlaunch and IGNITE your project!

John Lee Dumas
Multi-bestselling author and founder of Entrepreneur on Fire

I would highly recommend working with Chris. He's highly skilled had high integrity and produces great results.

Allan Dib
Bestselling author of The 1-Page Marketing Plan

Chris and his team at Jetlaunch did an amazing job with my latest book. I loved the professional design, and everyone on the team was friendly and helpful. I highly recommend JETLAUNCH. They are a joy to work with!

Dr Joe Vitale
Star in the hit movie, The Secret

I've hired Chris for dozens of projects. He is responsive, professional, and extremely competent. Chris and his team produce brilliant work.

Kary Oberbrunner
Multi-bestselling author and founder of Ethos Collective
publishing company

Jetlaunch is the real deal! They do not disappoint! Their design and communication skills are OVER THE TOP!

Wendy Bryant
Multi-bestselling author

Chris O'Byrne and his team were simply outstanding. When I was ready to go with my book project, the entire process flowed smoothly and seamlessly. Jetlaunch answered all my questions quickly and accurately. ETDBW (Easy To Do Business With) is the best description I can apply. They handled every detail professionally. My book looks terrific and I'm proud to give it to people (and it became an Amazon hot seller almost immediately on launch). Great people, great company.

Doug Kirkpatrick
Bestselling author and TEDx and keynote speaker

I am not even sure where to begin! Chris is an amazing man with an amazing company! His motivation to help others to "Serve" is one of his highest strengths! I highly value this man as a CEO, friend, and leader in the industry!

There are literally not enough pleasant words I can say about Chris and his team over at Jetlaunch! Loyalty to those he serves, respect always, selfless service to do the job right! One of the most honorable men I know! Gets the job done! Lastly to drop the mic! 15 international bestselling books to my name! All Chris! Thanks brother, I appreciate you! Hire him NOW!

Jason Miller
Multi-bestselling author, CEO of Strategic Advisor Board and several other companies

In my professional journey, few individuals have made as lasting an impression as Chris O'Byrne. His character is a blend of unwavering principles and a genuine warmth that makes collaborating with him a truly enriching experience. Chris's integrity is evident in every decision he makes, ensuring that fairness and transparency are at the forefront, creating an environment of trust and mutual respect.

What sets Chris apart is his visionary mindset. He has an innate ability to anticipate future trends and challenges, always thinking several steps ahead. This forward-thinking approach, combined with his deep industry knowledge, has been instrumental in charting new paths and pioneering innovative solutions. But vision alone isn't enough, and this is where Chris's exceptional execution skills come into play. He doesn't just set ambitious targets; he meticulously crafts strategies and mobilizes resources to ensure those targets are met, often surpassing expectations.

Joel Phillips
Multi-bestselling author and CEO of Proshark

I loved Jetlaunch's customer service. If I had a question, they were there to answer it. They guided me and were patient with me. Sometimes I wasn't sure what to do or I needed more time on a project, but they were there to support my needs. They also got back to me really quickly. I felt respect and that they cared about my project. Thank you so much, Jetlaunch!! ☺

Lynn Hoerauf
Multi-bestselling author

THE BOOK
WEALTH SYSTEM

TRANSFORM YOUR MARKETING WITH A
BUSINESS-BUILDING BOOK

Chris O'Byrne

18x International Bestselling Author and
Publisher of Over 15,000 Books

ISBN: 979-8-89079-163-4 (hardcover)
ISBN: 979-8-89079-164-1 (paperback)
ISBN: 979-8-89079-165-8 (ebook)

Jetlaunch Publishing

bookwealthsystem.com

Table of Contents

Don't Skip This!

Imagine waking up each day with a heavy feeling in your chest. No matter how hard you try, your business (and your dreams) feels stuck. It's like shouting into an empty space, hoping someone will hear you, but all you get back is silence. It's really frustrating, right? You remember when getting new customers seemed easy, but now it feels like they've disappeared, playing a game of hide and seek where you're always "it."

The reason for this pain is simple. The market is crowded, and standing out is harder than ever. You've tried all the usual advice, but it's just not working anymore. The business world changes fast; what worked yesterday might not work today. Without a clear message, your efforts get lost in the noise, making you feel invisible.

This struggle affects more than just your business. It causes money problems, leading to sleepless nights and constant worry. Your relationships—especially with those closest to you—feel strained. The stress and frustration make you doubt yourself and your business.

Now, imagine something different.

Picture a life where your business is thriving. Every day, you wake up excited, knowing you're moving forward. You've finally found a way to get more customers and make more money. Instead of your message falling on deaf ears, you have a steady stream of people who see the value in what you offer.

With this success, you can hire a team to help you, giving you time to relax and enjoy life. Imagine spending more time with your family or taking a week off without worrying about your business grinding to a halt. The stress disappears, replaced by relief and a sense of achievement. You feel proud and confident, talking about your business with joy, knowing you've built something great.

This transformation isn't just a dream; it's possible. I help people every day reach this goal, and I wrote this book to guide you every step of the way. It starts by helping you understand your business, your target audience, and your unique value. This understanding is the key to creating a message that stands out.

You'll learn easy strategies for getting more leads and creating marketing campaigns that connect with your ideal customers. This book also covers how to turn those leads into loyal customers through genuine engagement and valuable offers.

How is this possible? What's my big secret?

It's simple. All you need is a short book, just like this one. In fact, this book was designed not only to show you the way to a predictable lead-gen system but also to be a model you can copy. It's my *Book Wealth System*, and it can be yours as well.

Who am I to guide you and show you the way? I could give you a long rags-to-riches story or go on and on about how much I've accomplished, but I'll keep it short and simple. Through my company, Jetlaunch Publishing, I've helped publish over 15,000 books. Many of them became #1 *Wall Street Journal* bestsellers, and hundreds and hundreds became #1 Amazon bestsellers. This book you're reading right now is the 18th international bestselling book I've written. I've helped thousands of authors find success with nothing more than their book and a good marketing plan to leverage it. I call this *The Book Wealth System*.

By following the advice and using the strategies in this book, you'll overcome the obstacles holding your business back. You'll get the attention you deserve and build a successful business that stands out in today's crowded market. Your journey from frustration to success starts here. Let's make this dream your reality. Let me show you the way.

My sales pitch…

This book shows you how to write a book that generates leads and grows your business. It's also an example of that same type of book.

A book can't generate leads unless it convinces the reader to go to a landing page and provide their email in exchange for something valuable (also called a lead magnet).

I would love for you to go to bookwealthsystem.com/bonus and get a lead magnet I wrote and designed just for you. It's called *Discover 3 Proven Book Funnels That Effortlessly Convert Readers.*

Sound tempting? I hope so! In this book, I'll teach you how to use a book funnel to guide your ideal reader to book a call and become one of your ideal clients.

If you would like to see this in action, please go to bookwealthsystem.com/bonus to get your own copy of *Discover 3 Proven Book Funnels That Effortlessly Convert Readers.*

You can also use this QR code:

Introduction

Welcome to *The Book Wealth System*. I'm excited to share this journey with you. I'm excited to show you how your book can help you generate leads and grow your business. A book is one of the most powerful ways to establish yourself as an authority in your field, and it will open new opportunities for you and your business. It can also be the catalyst for creating many profitable partnerships. People will seek you out just to do business with you, and you'll find yourself having to choose which opportunities to pursue first.

How to Use This Book

This book is organized into three main sections: Book Writing 2.0, Book Publishing 2.0, and Book Launch 2.0. Each section will guide you through a different stage of the book creation process. If you're just starting, begin with Book Writing 2.0. If you've already written your book, you might want to skip ahead to Book Publishing 2.0. And if you're ready to launch or re-launch, go straight to Book Launch 2.0.

The Power of a Book in Business

You might wonder how a book can help your business. A book is a powerful marketing tool. It will help you establish credibility, reach a wider audience, and create lasting connections with your readers. Many successful entrepreneurs have used books to grow their businesses. For example, Tim Ferriss used

The 4-Hour Workweek to build his brand and launch multiple ventures. Tony Robbins didn't become a household name until he published his first book. Your book will position you as an authority in your field, generate thousands of leads, and lead to speaking engagements and other high-impact opportunities.

Overview of *The Book Wealth System*

The Book Wealth System

Book Launch 2.0

Book Publishing 2.0

Book Writing 2.0

Each section of *The Book Wealth System* contains valuable information for that specific part of the process. In Book Writing 2.0, you'll learn how to craft a book that speaks directly and powerfully to your ideal clients. Book Publishing 2.0 guides you through the publishing process, including choosing the right publishing options, preparing your manuscript, and designing a professional book cover. Finally, Book Launch 2.0 shows you how to plan your book launch, build a launch team, create buzz, and leverage your book for long-term success. Each section is designed to help you at different stages of your book journey, but they all work together to help you achieve the overall goal of generating leads through your book and rapidly growing your business.

Setting Expectations

Before we get started, it's important to set realistic expectations. Writing, publishing, and launching a book requires time, effort, and dedication when you do it all yourself. By following the steps in this book, you can achieve great results. Remember that consistency and persistence are key. Don't be discouraged if things don't happen overnight. Take actionable steps after each chapter and keep moving forward. This process is a marathon, not a sprint. And remember, the Jetlaunch team is always here to carry the burden for you. We can write your book, design and publish, and even set up your entire book marketing system for you, including designing opt-in pages, lead magnets, and writing email sequences that turn readers into clients.

Preparing for Your Journey

As you embark on this journey, preparing your mindset is essential. Writing a book requires commitment and dedication. You might face challenges along the way, but stay focused on your goals. Stay motivated by reminding yourself why you started this journey. Surround yourself with supportive people who encourage you. Do not be afraid to ask for help when you need it. This book will provide you with the necessary tools and guidance, but your commitment and perseverance will ultimately drive your success. Let's get started on this exciting journey together.

SECTION 1

Book Writing 2.0

This section is all about creating a book that grabs attention, delivers value, and sets the foundation for your business success. Writing isn't just about putting words on a page; it's about crafting a message that speaks directly to your audience. These steps will show you how to create a book that makes readers take notice and want to learn more about what you offer.

The New Age of Book Writing introduces modern ways to write a book faster and more effectively. You'll learn how to use tools and strategies that make the process easier and more efficient.

Finding Your Book's Purpose helps you figure out why you're writing your book and who it's for. This step ensures your book has a clear goal and speaks to the right audience.

Crafting a Compelling Narrative focuses on storytelling techniques that keep readers interested. A great story keeps your audience engaged and makes your message memorable.

Writing with Clarity and Authority shows you how to communicate your ideas in a way that's easy to understand and shows your expertise. Readers trust a book that is clear and confident.

Overcoming Writer's Block gives you practical tips for staying motivated and pushing through challenges. You'll learn how to keep writing, even when it feels tough.

By the end of this section, you'll know how to write a book that connects with your readers and builds trust in your brand. These steps will guide you through creating a well-written book that's a powerful tool for growing your business.

Book Writing 2.0

Writing impactful, engaging books

Purposeful Writing

Identify your book's purpose and audience to ensure it has a clear goal and resonates well.

Engaging Storytelling

Incorporate compelling narrative techniques to keep readers hooked and your message unforgettable.

Efficient Writing Techniques

Use modern strategies to write faster and more efficiently, enhancing the overall book creation process.

Clarifying Ideas

Present your ideas clearly and authoritatively, which builds reader trust and comprehension.

Reader Engagement

Focus on creating content that grabs attention and maintains reader interest throughout the book.

Overcoming Writer's Block

Utilize practical methods to stay motivated and persist through challenges, even when writing feels difficult.

CHAPTER 1

The New Age of Book Writing

Overview of Book Writing 2.0

In today's digital age, book writing has evolved significantly. Gone are the days when authors had to rely solely on traditional publishing houses to get their work out to the public. With modern technology and various platforms at our disposal, the process has become more accessible and flexible. This new approach, which I like to call Book Writing 2.0, harnesses these advancements to make writing and publishing more efficient and impactful.

Leveraging modern technology means you can write, edit, and publish books faster than ever before. There are many tools that make it easier to organize your thoughts, correct mistakes, and format your manuscript. You can collaborate with people around the world without leaving your home. Self-publishing platforms like Amazon KDP (Kindle Direct Publishing) and IngramSpark allow you to bypass traditional gatekeepers and bring your book directly to your ideal reader.

However, it's not just about the tools you use; it's also about the methods you adopt. In the past, writing a book often took years. Today, you can adopt a more strategic approach. You can streamline the writing process by planning your content with clear goals and leveraging tools like artificial intelligence. You don't even need to write your book. You can record yourself speaking and create decent transcriptions for little to no extra cost. This shift from traditional to innovative methods enables you to produce a high-quality book that generates leads and grows your business.

Benefits of Writing a Book for Lead Generation

Book as a Business Tool

Authority Establishment · Personal Branding · Marketing Tool

Your book can be your most powerful tool for growing your business. One of the biggest benefits of writing a book is that it helps establish your authority and credibility in your industry. When you publish a book, you position yourself as an expert.

People are more likely to trust your knowledge and will want your services or products. This credibility can open doors to speaking engagements, media interviews, and other opportunities that further enhance your reputation.

A book also helps build your personal brand and expand your reach. By sharing your insights and experiences, you create a deeper connection with your readers. They get to know you, your values, and your approach. This connection is invaluable because it builds loyalty and trust. When people feel they know you, they are more likely to follow your advice, buy your products, or hire your services.

Moreover, a book serves as a powerful marketing tool. It attracts and engages leads in ways that other forms of content can't. A book provides value upfront, which helps attract potential customers. Once they've read your book, they are more likely to become paying clients because they've already benefited from your expertise.

Being a published author also offers long-term benefits. Your book will continue to generate leads and sales for years. It can be a foundational piece of content that supports your business growth over time. Plus, the credibility and authority that come with being an author can have a lasting impact on your career and business.

Writing a book offers numerous advantages. By leveraging modern technology and adopting innovative methods, you can make the writing process more efficient and effective. Once your book is published, it can help you establish authority, build your brand, attract and engage leads, and provide long-term benefits for your business.

Sarah had a dream of writing a book but felt overwhelmed by the traditional process. She didn't have the time or energy to sit and write for hours. I introduced her to Book Writing 2.0, where she could record her thoughts and have them transcribed instead of writing by hand. By using AI tools for editing and organizing, we cut her production time in half. Within a few weeks, we published her book on Amazon, and it became a strong lead magnet for her coaching business. The book made her an expert in her field and attracted new clients who trusted her methods.

Now that you understand the modern approach to writing a book, it's time to focus on the most important question: Why are you writing this book in the first place? In the next chapter, we'll dive into how to find your book's purpose and identify the audience you want to reach. With a clear goal and the right readers in mind, you'll be ready to create a book that truly makes an impact.

How to Write Your Book in the New Age of Book Writing

1. Streamline Writing with Modern Tools

Writing a book can feel overwhelming, but tools like Scrivener, Google Docs, and Otter.ai make the process easier and faster. These technologies help you organize your thoughts, transcribe spoken ideas, and produce a polished manuscript. If you're feeling stuck, try recording your ideas and transcribing them—it's a great way to break through writer's block while staying productive.

2. Focus on Solving Your Readers' Problems

Your audience is looking for solutions. Plan your book with clear goals, addressing their specific pain points. For instance, if your readers struggle with marketing their business, structure your book to deliver actionable strategies they can implement immediately. This focus ensures your book resonates with their needs and establishes you as the expert they can trust.

3. Break the Process into Small, Achievable Goals

Writing a book doesn't have to consume your life. Set manageable goals like writing 500 words a day or completing a chapter outline each week. These small steps add up quickly and keep you moving forward. One client, Sarah, used this method and completed her book in just eight weeks, all while managing a full-time business.

4. Engage Readers with Relatable Stories

Stories make your book memorable. Share real-life examples or client success stories that illustrate your points. For example, instead of saying, "Streamlining your writing is possible," tell the story of Mark, who used AI tools to turn his scattered ideas into a cohesive book, growing his business by 30 percent within six months.

5. Get Feedback to Stay on Track

Don't write in isolation. Share drafts with peers, beta readers, or a trusted editor to ensure your book resonates with its intended audience. Tools like Grammarly can help with grammar and style, but real feedback from others will give you clarity on how your book connects emotionally and practically with readers.

By following these steps, you'll not only write your book efficiently but also ensure it speaks directly to your audience's needs. Start today—outline your first chapter or try recording a short section. Each step you take brings you closer to a professional book that sets you apart as a leader in your field.

CHAPTER 2

Finding Your Book's Purpose

Identifying Your Target Audience

When I started writing my book, I knew I had to figure out who my target audience was. Without understanding who you're writing for, it's like throwing darts in the dark. The first step I took was conducting market research. This doesn't have to be complicated. I began by looking at my current customers and clients. Who were they? What problems did they have? What solutions were they looking for? This gave me a basic idea of who my readers might be.

I wanted to understand my ideal clients better, so I asked several of them about their biggest pain points and what they hoped their life would be like once those pains were gone. I listened closely to their stories and paid attention to the exact words they used to describe their problems and dreams. This helped me see their challenges and hopes more clearly. By using their words, I could connect with them more genuinely and create strategies that addressed their needs and wants. This way, the solutions I provided felt like they were made just for them (and they were).

Defining the Goals for Your Book

Once I had a clear picture of my audience, I defined the goals for my book. It's important to set clear objectives for what you want to achieve. For me, the main goal was to generate leads for my business. While that's not the only goal a book can have, all books should incorporate some form of lead generation. Whatever your goals are, write them down and keep them in mind as you work.

Aligning the book's goals with my business strategy was also crucial. I wanted the book to complement my other marketing efforts and fit into my overall business plan. For instance, if your business offers consulting services, your book could be a way to showcase your expertise and attract new clients. Make sure the goals of your book support and enhance your business strategy.

It's also essential to balance lead generation with providing value to your readers. Yes, you want to attract new leads, but you also want to give your readers something of real value. If your book feels like a sales pitch, it won't resonate. Focus on solving a problem or answering a question your readers have, and the leads will follow naturally.

Clarifying Your Message and Unique Selling Proposition (USP)

With my audience and goals in mind, the next step was to clarify my message and unique selling proposition (USP). The core message of your book is what you want your readers to take away after they finish reading. It should be simple, clear, and impactful. For example, my core message was that anyone can write a book to grow their business, regardless of their writing experience.

Differentiating your book from others in the market is also key. There are probably a lot of books out there on the same topic you're writing about. So, what makes yours different? It could be your unique perspective, your personal experiences, or the specific strategies you offer. Think about what sets your book apart and make that a central part of your marketing.

Crafting a compelling USP that resonates with readers ties everything together. Your USP should communicate the main benefit of your book in a way that grabs attention. It's not just about what your book is about but why someone should read it. For example, "Publish a book in 90 days that attracts customers and grows your business, even if you've never written a book." That's a USP that speaks directly to a specific need and promises a clear benefit.

Finding your book's purpose starts with understanding who you're writing for and what you want to achieve. By identifying your target audience, defining your goals, and clarifying your message and USP, you can create a book that attracts leads and provides real value to your readers.

Book Creation Strategy

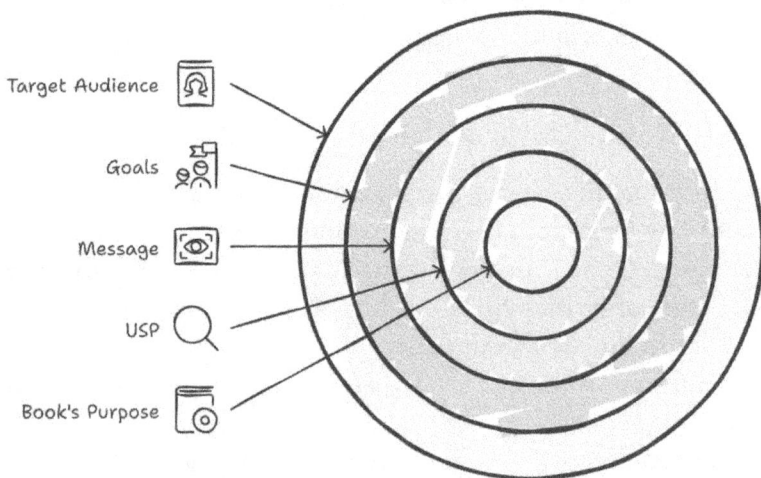

Target Audience

Goals

Message

USP

Book's Purpose

One of my clients, Mark, was having a hard time figuring out the purpose of his book. He knew he wanted to grow his financial consulting business but wasn't sure how to shape the book to help with that. I helped him identify his target audience by looking at his current clients and their biggest problems. We realized that his ideal readers were small business owners who needed help managing cash flow.

Together, we set the book's goal: to generate leads for his consulting services while giving small business owners practical advice about managing cash flow. I helped him clarify his message by focusing on simple strategies for improving cash flow, which became his unique selling point. In the end, his book connected with his audience and positioned him as an expert, bringing in a steady flow of new clients.

Now that you've identified your book's purpose and audience, it's time to make your message come alive. In the next chapter, we'll explore how to craft a compelling narrative that keeps readers hooked from start to finish. By using the power of storytelling, you'll create a book that not only informs but also inspires and connects with your audience.

How to Define Your Book's Purpose

1. Understand Your Audience's Struggles

To write a book that resonates, start by understanding what your audience is going through. Use tools like surveys, social media polls, or direct conversations with clients to uncover their biggest pain points. For example, ask open-ended questions like, "What challenges keep you up at night?" Pay attention to recurring themes, as these insights will guide your book's focus. Understanding their struggles ensures you're solving the problems they care about most.

2. Set Clear Goals for Your Book

Define what you want your book to achieve for both you and your readers. Is your goal to generate leads, establish your authority, or provide actionable solutions? Write these goals down and revisit them often to stay on track. For example, if your primary goal is to generate leads, structure your chapters with calls-to-action that naturally encourage readers to connect with you. A clear purpose ensures your book delivers measurable results.

3. Develop Your Unique Selling Proposition (USP)

Stand out from the crowd by identifying what makes your book unique. Look at similar books in your niche and determine how yours offers something different. For instance, if other books provide general advice, yours could focus on a specific audience, like "Time Management for Busy Moms." Highlight your USP in your title, introduction, and throughout the book. This will make your book memorable and compelling.

4. Describe the Transformation Your Book Provides

Paint a vivid picture of how your reader's life will change after applying your advice. For example, if your book is about personal finance, describe how readers can go from living paycheck to paycheck to confidently managing their money. Use relatable language that speaks directly to their aspirations. This transformation becomes the emotional hook that keeps readers engaged and motivated.

5. Plan the Reader's Next Step

Don't leave readers wondering what to do after finishing your book. Include actionable next steps, like visiting a website, downloading a free resource, or scheduling a consultation. For example, "Download my free budgeting template at [your website] to start applying these principles today." By providing a clear path forward, you'll turn readers into loyal followers or clients.

CHAPTER 3

Crafting a Compelling Narrative

When it comes to writing your lead-gen book, storytelling is a powerful tool. Even though we're dealing with facts and real-life events, weaving them into a narrative can make the information much more engaging. Think about the difference between reading a dry manual and a compelling memoir. Both might offer useful insights, but one keeps you turning the pages while the other might put you to sleep.

The first thing to understand is that storytelling is about more than just presenting information. It's about creating an experience for the reader. I like to structure my books with a narrative arc to do this. This means starting with an introduction that sets the stage, building up to a climax where the most exciting or critical information is presented, and then wrapping things up with a conclusion that ties everything together. This structure helps keep readers engaged from start to finish.

Incorporating real-life examples and case studies is another effective storytelling technique. People love stories about other people. Sharing real-life examples makes the content more relatable and helps illustrate your points in a concrete way. When I was writing my book, I included stories from my experiences and those of my clients. These stories helped bring the concepts to life and showed how the ideas I was discussing played out in the real world.

Structuring Your Book for Maximum Impact

I spent a lot of time focusing on the structure to ensure my book had the maximum impact. Outlining the chapters and sub-sections was the first step. An outline serves as a roadmap for your book, helping you stay organized and focused. Each chapter should build on the previous one, leading the reader on a logical journey through your content.

Using frameworks and models to organize the content can also be very helpful. Frameworks provide a structure that can make complex information easier to digest. For example, I used a simple three-part framework in my book to explain the process of writing, publishing, and launching a book. This makes the information more manageable for readers and gives them a clear path to follow.

Ensuring logical flow and coherence throughout the book is crucial. Each chapter should flow naturally into the next, and the ideas should connect in a way that makes sense. I like to think of my book as a conversation with the reader. Each chapter is a new topic in that conversation, but the overall discussion remains connected and cohesive.

Balancing Information and Engagement

One of the biggest challenges in writing your lead-gen book is balancing valuable information with engaging writing. It's important to provide useful insights and practical advice, but you also want to keep the reader interested. To do this, I focus on combining solid information with engaging writing techniques.

Making complex topics accessible is key. I aim to explain things in simple terms without assuming the reader has prior knowledge of the subject. Breaking down complex ideas into smaller, more digestible parts can help. For example, when discussing a complicated concept, I might start with a basic explanation and then gradually add more detail.

Using anecdotes and personal stories is another way to keep the reader engaged. People connect with stories on an emotional level, so sharing personal experiences can make the content more relatable and interesting. In this book, I include stories about my journey as a publisher and the challenges my clients and I have faced along the way. These anecdotes help illustrate my points and add a personal touch to the book.

Blending storytelling techniques, a solid structure, and engaging writing, I crafted a compelling narrative that kept readers interested while providing them with valuable information. Writing a lead-gen book that people want to read is about more than just sharing facts; it's about telling a story that informs, engages, and inspires.

Elements of Compelling Writing

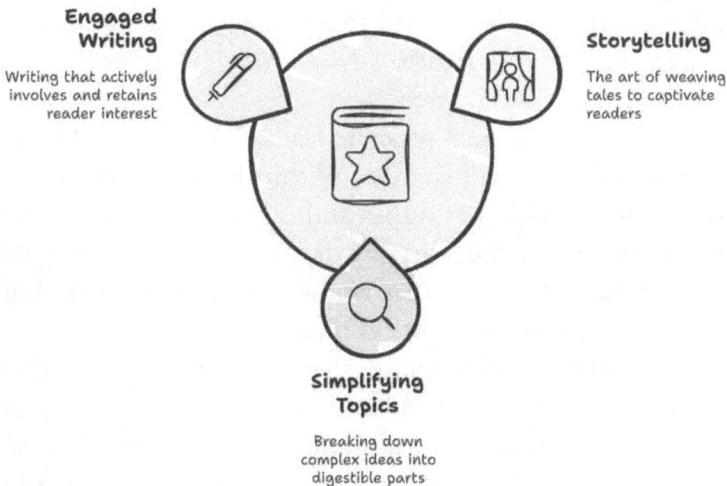

Engaged Writing

Writing that actively involves and retains reader interest

Storytelling

The art of weaving tales to captivate readers

Simplifying Topics

Breaking down complex ideas into digestible parts

When Lisa came to me, she was frustrated. Her lead-gen book was packed with great information, but she worried it read like a dry manual instead of a page-turner that would hook her readers and drive business. She asked, "How do I make this *not boring?*"

I told her, "Think of your book like a dinner party. Facts are the main course, but stories are the spices that make the meal memorable." Together, we created a simple structure: start by showing the reader you understand their struggles, guide them to see how your solutions work, and close with clear, actionable steps they can take.

To bring it to life, we added real client stories. For example, instead of saying, "X strategy works," Lisa shared how a client once called her in tears, overwhelmed by a failing project, and how implementing her strategy turned things around. Suddenly, readers weren't just learning from Lisa; they were rooting for her clients and engaged in their stories.

We also wove in unconventional hooks, like mini case studies and "what if" scenarios, to keep readers engaged. Lisa's book went from a sleepy read to a dynamic tool that felt like a conversation with a trusted advisor. Readers connected with her expertise *and* her humanity.

Her book didn't just generate leads; it positioned her as a relatable authority in her field. Within months, Lisa saw an increase in consulting inquiries and opportunities to speak at industry events. By transforming dry facts into compelling stories, Lisa created a book that worked harder for her business than any marketing brochure ever could.

With your narrative taking shape, it's important to make sure your writing is clear and authoritative. In the next chapter, we'll focus on how to communicate your ideas effectively, ensuring your readers understand and trust what you have to say. This will help you build credibility and make your book truly impactful.

How to Craft a Compelling Narrative

1. Use a Clear Story Structure

A strong narrative starts with structure. Introduce the problem your audience faces, guide them through a journey of discovery, and conclude with a resolution that inspires action. For example, begin with a relatable struggle like difficulty finding clients, and end with a clear strategy that leads to success. This arc keeps readers engaged and gives your content emotional depth.

2. Share Relatable Examples

Stories make abstract ideas real. Include specific examples of people or businesses who have used your advice successfully. For instance, instead of saying, "You can grow your sales," describe how one client doubled their revenue in three months by applying your methods. Relatable examples help readers see how they, too, can achieve similar results.

3. Make the Reader the Hero

While your expertise guides them, position the reader as the hero of the story. Show how your strategies empower them to overcome challenges and achieve transformation. Use language like, "You can take these steps to..." rather than "I recommend..." This approach puts the spotlight on your reader and reinforces their ability to succeed.

4. Write in a Conversational Tone

Avoid overly formal or technical language that could alienate readers. Instead, write as if you're speaking to a friend, keeping the tone warm and approachable. For example, rather than saying, "Implement these methodologies," say, "Here's an easy way to make this work for you." A conversational tone builds trust and makes your book more enjoyable.

5. Add Emotional Hooks

Emotion drives action. Include moments in your writing that evoke feelings of hope, relief, or excitement. For instance, share a story of a client who turned their business around against all odds. These emotional elements inspire readers to stay engaged and take action based on your advice.

CHAPTER 4

Writing with Clarity and Authority

Techniques for Clear and Engaging Writing

When I set out to write my book, I knew that writing clearly and engagingly was essential. If your readers can't easily understand what you're saying, they'll lose interest quickly. One of the first things I focused on was keeping my writing clear and concise. This meant getting to the point without unnecessary fluff. Each sentence needed to serve a purpose. I also found it helpful to avoid jargon and overly technical language. It's easy to fall into the trap of using industry-specific terms, but that can alienate readers who aren't familiar with them. Instead, I aimed to write in a way that anyone could understand, regardless of their background.

Readability was another key factor. I wanted my book to be easy to read and digest. Short sentences and paragraphs helped achieve this. Breaking down complex ideas into simpler components made the content more accessible. Whenever I introduced a new concept, I provided examples to illustrate my points. This way, readers could see how the ideas are applied in real-world situations.

Steps to Clear and Engaging Writing

Clear & Concise

Avoid Jargon

Enhance Readability

Simplify Ideas

Use Examples

Establishing Your Voice and Expertise

Finding and developing your voice is one of the most critical aspects of writing a book, especially one meant to market your business and establish credibility. Your voice is what makes your writing uniquely yours; it's how you connect with readers authentically and consistently. Writing in a conversational tone, as if speaking directly to the reader, feels most natural to me. This approach doesn't just make the writing more engaging; it also builds a sense of trust and relatability.

Early in my career, I struggled with this. I felt immense pressure to be "professional" in everything I wrote, thinking I had to prove myself to be taken seriously. However, in trying so hard to fit a mold, I ended up feeling—and sounding—inauthentic. It was exhausting and out of sync with the person I wanted to be.

Over time, as I gained experience and confidence, I stopped trying to be what I thought others expected and started focusing on who I really was. I began writing in my true voice, communicating authentically and consistently, and the results were transformative. My writing felt more honest, and my audience connected with me on a deeper level. This journey changed my approach and gave me the skills to help others find their voices, even when they feel stuck or uncertain.

Equally important in your book is showcasing your expertise. Readers need to trust you know your stuff. By sharing your experiences, insights, and lessons learned, you add credibility to your advice. It's all about balance: You can't just be the expert; you must also be relatable. Including personal stories and even admitting past mistakes can make you more approachable and human.

Your expertise is the foundation of your authority, but your voice is the bridge that connects you to your audience. A great book isn't just about what you know; it's about how you make readers feel as they learn from you. That balance of authenticity and authority is what transforms a book into a powerful tool for your business.

Editing and Refining Your Manuscript

Editing and refining your manuscript is crucial to improving clarity and coherence. Do not edit your own manuscript! I've been editing for over twenty years and have eighteen international bestselling books, and I will not edit my books. I know better. Hiring a professional editor will elevate your manuscript to a higher standard.

Writing with clarity and authority is about making your content accessible and ensuring your expertise shines through. It's a process that involves careful planning, continuous refinement, and a commitment to connecting with your readers in a meaningful way. By focusing on clear writing, developing a strong voice, and thorough editing, you can create a book that resonates with your audience, establishes you as a credible author, and, best of all, helps you grow your business.

Andy struggled to make his writing clear and engaging. He had a wealth of knowledge in his field but found it hard to explain his ideas without using complex jargon. I helped him simplify his language and focus on his core message. Together, we trimmed down unnecessary details and worked on making his sentences more concise.

We also found ways to break down complicated concepts into digestible pieces with real-world examples, which made his book easier to follow. As a result, Andy's writing became clearer and more relatable, helping him connect better with his readers. His book positioned him as an expert and attracted more clients to his business.

Now that you know how to write with clarity and authority, it's time to tackle one of the biggest challenges for any writer: staying motivated. In the next chapter, we'll explore practical ways to overcome writer's block so you can keep your momentum and finish your book with confidence.

How to Write with Clarity and Authority

1. Simplify Complex Ideas

Break down complicated topics into simple, easy-to-follow steps. Use plain language and avoid jargon. For instance, instead of saying, "Utilize multi-channel attribution modeling," say, "Track where your customers are coming from and adjust your strategies accordingly." Simplicity ensures readers understand your points without frustration.

2. Organize Your Content Logically

Structure your book in a way that makes it easy for readers to follow. Start with foundational concepts, build on them with examples, and end with actionable advice. Use headings, subheadings, and bullet points to guide readers. For example, a chapter on marketing could include sections like "Understanding Your Audience" and "Creating Campaigns That Convert."

3. Back Up Your Claims

Establish authority by supporting your advice with evidence. Include statistics, studies, or quotes from experts. For example, "According to a recent study, businesses using email marketing saw a 30 percent increase in sales." This not only builds trust but also reinforces your credibility as an author.

4. Develop Your Unique Voice

Your voice sets you apart. Whether it's humorous, empathetic, or authoritative, let your personality shine through your writing. For example, if you're naturally encouraging, weave motivational language into your advice. A distinct voice makes your book memorable and relatable.

5. Get Feedback and Edit Thoroughly

Even the best writers benefit from feedback. Share drafts with peers or beta readers to ensure your message is clear and impactful. Professional editing is essential to catch errors and refine your work. Polished writing shows respect for your audience and enhances your credibility.

CHAPTER 5

Avoid Writer's Block by Not Writing

Understanding and Identifying Writer's Block

Every writer, no matter how experienced, hits a wall sometimes. Writer's block is a common obstacle, and understanding it can help you overcome it. For me, writer's block often comes from a mix of fear and perfectionism—fear that my writing won't be good enough and a desire to make every sentence perfect on the first try. These feelings can be paralyzing.

Another cause can be feeling overwhelmed by the project. Staring at a blank page or a massive outline can make it hard to know where to start. Sometimes, it's a lack of inspiration; the ideas just don't seem to flow. Recognizing these signs early is crucial because they can significantly slow down your writing process. When I find myself avoiding writing, procrastinating, or feeling anxious about getting started, I know writer's block is setting in.

Strategies to Maintain Writing Momentum

One of the most effective ways I've found to combat writer's block is by setting realistic writing goals and deadlines. Instead of aiming to write an entire chapter in one sitting, I break it down into smaller, more manageable tasks. For instance, I might set a goal to write 500 words a day. This keeps the momentum going and makes the task feel less daunting. Meeting these smaller goals provides a sense of accomplishment that keeps me motivated.

Creating a conducive writing environment also plays a big role. I set up a dedicated writing space free from distractions. This doesn't have to be fancy; it could be a quiet corner of your home or a local coffee shop. The key is to find a place where you can focus. I also make sure to have everything I need within reach, like my notes, a good chair, and a cup of coffee.

Developing a regular writing routine is essential. I try to write at the same time every day. This consistency trains my brain to expect to write, making it easier to get into the flow. Whether it's early in the morning or late at night, finding a time that works best for you and sticking to it can make a huge difference.

Tools and Resources to Support Your Writing Process

There are many tools and resources available that can help boost productivity and keep you on track. Some people use apps like Word, Scrivener, and Google Docs. Others enjoy joining groups that help them connect with other writers and stay accountable. My favorite writing tool, however, is a voice recorder. That's right; I prefer not to write my books but to record them instead.

First, I write a general outline or table of contents. I start with a birds-eye view. Next, I expand on each of those entries and create a detailed outline. After that feels right for my overall goals for the book, I start recording. Without the outline, I would ramble, and the book would feel unorganized and painful to read. The outline keeps me focused so I can record shorter sections and still stay on track. After recording, I upload the audio to a transcription service, clean up the text I receive, and then send it to my editor to finish.

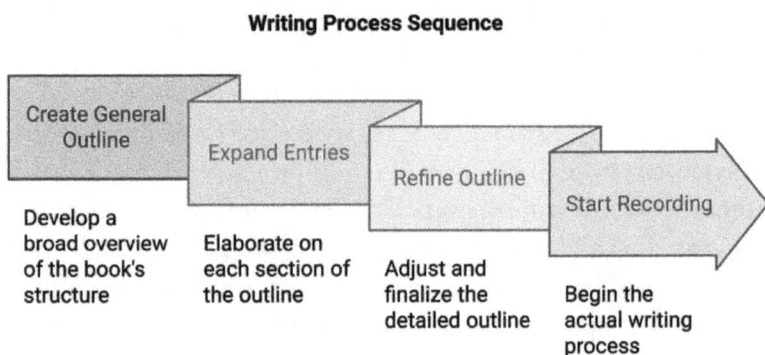

Writing Process Sequence

Create General Outline	Expand Entries	Refine Outline	Start Recording
Develop a broad overview of the book's structure	Elaborate on each section of the outline	Adjust and finalize the detailed outline	Begin the actual writing process

However, both writing and recording take a lot of time. If you are a business owner, your time is better spent working on your business and hiring a professional to write your book for you. It's more cost effective, also. Books designed to generate leads and grow your business require skills and acumen that most people don't possess, even ghostwriters. It requires a unique blend of understanding both writing and marketing, along with copywriting and customer psychology.

Tom was experiencing severe writer's block while working on his book. He felt overwhelmed by the size of the project and had no idea where to start. Instead of forcing him to sit down and write, I suggested he try recording his thoughts. We started by creating a clear outline to guide him, breaking his ideas into smaller sections. Then, he recorded each section while following the outline.

This approach allowed Tom to bypass the pressure of writing and freed up his creativity. After having his recordings transcribed, we cleaned up the text and sent it to my editor. Not only did this method save him time, but it also helped him finish his book without the frustration of writer's block. His book is now a key tool in generating leads for his business, all while he spent more time focusing on his clients.

With your writing process underway, it's time to think about what comes next: publishing your book. The next section will explore modern publishing options and help you decide the best path to bring your book to life. Whether you choose self-publishing or a traditional route, this step will set the stage for reaching your audience.

How to Overcome Writer's Block

1. Start with an Outline

Writer's block often stems from uncertainty about where to start. Combat this by creating a detailed outline of your book. Break it into chapters, and within each chapter, list key points to cover. For example, in a chapter on marketing, include sections like "Audience Research" and "Campaign Creation." An outline gives structure, making it easier to write with confidence.

2. Set Small, Achievable Goals

Writing an entire book can feel overwhelming, so focus on small, daily goals. Instead of aiming for a full chapter in one sitting, commit to writing 500 words or one section each day. These smaller milestones are easier to manage and keep you motivated as you see steady progress toward your final draft.

3. Record Your Thoughts Instead of Writing

If you're struggling to write, speak your ideas out loud. Use a voice recorder or tools like Otter.ai to capture your thoughts and transcribe them into text. This approach works especially well if you're a verbal communicator. You can focus on refining the transcription later, freeing yourself from the pressure of perfect writing upfront.

4. Change Your Writing Environment

A change in scenery can work wonders for your creativity. If you usually write at your desk, try a quiet coffee shop, a library, or even your backyard. Shifting your surroundings can spark new ideas and help you refocus. Many writers find that being in a new space energizes their creativity and breaks mental blocks.

5. Accept Imperfection in the First Draft

One of the biggest causes of writer's block is perfectionism. Remind yourself that your first draft is just a starting point and doesn't have to be perfect. Focus on getting your ideas down without worrying about grammar or style. Once the draft is complete, you can refine and polish it during editing.

SECTION 2

Book Publishing 2.0

In this section, you'll learn how to get your book ready for the world and make it stand out. Publishing isn't just about printing a book; it's about creating something that looks professional and appeals to your audience. These steps will guide you through the process of getting your book into readers' hands and making it a success.

Understanding Modern Publishing Options explores the different ways to publish your book, from self-publishing to traditional methods. You'll learn which option fits your goals and how to get started.

Preparing Your Manuscript focuses on making your book look polished and professional. This step ensures your words are clear, well-organized, and ready for readers.

Designing a Professional Book Cover highlights the importance of a great cover. A good cover grabs attention and makes people want to pick up your book.

Publishing Platforms and Distribution explains how to get your book on the platforms where readers are looking, like Amazon or bookstores. You'll also learn how to reach a wider audience.

Pricing and Royalties helps you decide how much to charge for your book and explains how you'll earn money from it. Setting the right price is key to attracting buyers while meeting your business goals.

By following these steps, you'll be ready to publish a book that looks professional, reaches your audience, and supports your business. This section will help you bring your book to life and share it with the world.

Book Publishing 2.0

Modern Publishing Options

Explore self-publishing and traditional methods to select the best fit for your publishing goals.

Professional Book Cover Design

A compelling cover is crucial for grabbing attention and increasing book sales.

Manuscript Preparation

Ensure clear, organized content that presents a polished, professional, ready-to-read manuscript for your audience.

Platform and Distribution

Learn to place your book on popular platforms like Amazon to maximize audience reach.

Understanding Royalties

Learn how much you'll earn per sale and incorporate this into your pricing strategy.

Pricing Strategies

Set a competitive price that balances profit and marketability for your book.

CHAPTER 6

Why Traditional Publishing Isn't Worth It for Business Growth

Impact on Lead Generation

If your goal is to turn readers into clients and grow your business, traditional publishing might not be the best option. When you publish through a traditional publisher, they often have strict rules about what you can include in your book. These rules can prevent you from adding direct calls-to-action (CTAs) or links to your website, which are essential for generating leads.

In contrast, self-publishing lets you decide exactly what to include. You can strategically place CTAs throughout your book, guiding readers to your website, sign-up forms, or directly to your services. Without these CTAs, your book won't be as effective at turning readers into clients. Traditional publishers may also limit how much promotional content you can include, making it harder to use your book as a tool to drive business growth.

Customization and Personalization

Another key aspect of using a book to grow your business is making sure the content speaks directly to your audience. With traditional publishing, editors might make changes that could water down your message or make it too generic. This can be a problem if your goal is to connect with a specific group of people who need your services.

Self-publishing gives you the flexibility to tailor your book's content to your audience's needs. You can include personal stories, industry-specific advice, and tips that resonate with your readers. This customization makes your book more relevant and engaging, increasing the chances that readers will see you as an expert who understands their challenges.

Plus, with self-publishing, you can quickly update your content if your business changes or you gain new insights. With its long editing and production process, traditional publishing doesn't offer this kind of flexibility, meaning your content could be outdated by the time it reaches your audience.

Building an Email List

Building an email list is one of the most valuable things you can do with a book. An email list lets you stay in touch with your readers, nurture leads over time, and eventually turn them into clients. However, traditional publishers often restrict where and how you can include invitations for readers to join your email list in your book.

Self-publishing gives you complete control over how you capture leads. You can place offers for free resources, exclusive content, or discounts throughout your book to encourage readers to share their email addresses. You can also test different approaches and tweak your offers in real-time based on what works best—something traditional publishing doesn't easily allow.

Building an email list through your book creates a long-term asset that continuously benefits your business. You can engage with your readers through newsletters, special offers, and personalized content, keeping them connected to your brand long after they finish your book.

Direct Feedback and Engagement

Engaging with your readers is crucial when building a business through book publishing. Self-publishing lets you maintain a direct connection with your audience so you can receive and respond to feedback immediately. Readers can reach out to you directly through the contact information you include in your book or through the platforms where your book is published. This feedback is invaluable for understanding what resonates with your audience and what you could improve in future editions.

Traditional publishing often puts a barrier between you and your readers since the publisher usually controls much of the communication. This separation can prevent you from engaging with your readers on a personal level, missing opportunities to build relationships, address concerns, or gather insights that could shape your business strategies.

Self-publishing not only allows this direct engagement but also encourages it. You can respond to reader reviews, participate in discussions, and even incorporate reader suggestions into future work. This ongoing dialogue helps build a community around your book and your brand, fostering loyalty and trust among your audience.

If your goal is to grow your business by using your book to generate leads, traditional publishing doesn't offer the flexibility, control, or direct engagement opportunities that self-publishing does. By self-publishing, you can customize your content, actively build your email list, and maintain a meaningful connection with your readers—all critical elements for turning readers into clients and driving your business forward.

Pathways to Success

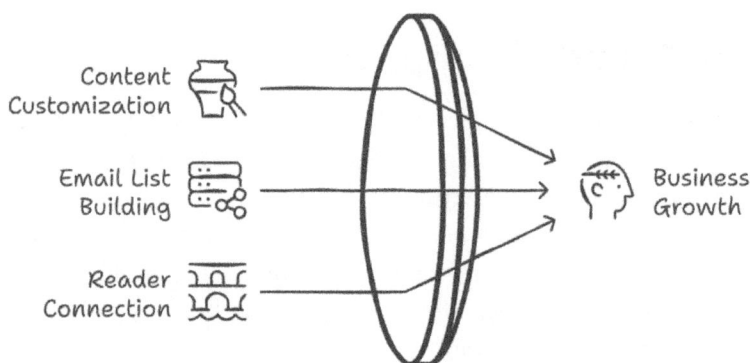

I worked with James, who initially planned to publish his book through a traditional publisher to grow his business. However, after discussing his goals, it became clear that the restrictions of traditional publishing wouldn't work for him. He needed to include calls-to-action and direct links to his services throughout his book to turn readers into clients.

I helped James self-publish his book instead, allowing him to place strategic CTAs and links that guided readers to his website and sign-up forms. This approach helped him build his email list and generate a steady flow of leads. Within months of publishing, James saw an increase in new clients, all thanks to the control and flexibility self-publishing provided.

Now that you understand your publishing options, it's time to prepare your manuscript for success. In the next chapter, we'll focus on getting your book ready for publication, from editing and formatting to ensuring it looks professional. This step is crucial to making a great impression on your readers.

How to Choose the Right Publishing Path

1. Research Self-Publishing Platforms

Self-publishing offers control over your content, pricing, and distribution. Platforms like Amazon KDP and IngramSpark allow you to publish quickly and access large audiences. For example, Amazon KDP lets you publish ebooks and paperbacks with global reach. Research each platform's features, costs, and royalties to determine which aligns best with your goals.

2. Evaluate the Pros and Cons of Traditional Publishing

Traditional publishing provides access to experienced editors, marketing resources, and established distribution channels. However, it often requires relinquishing creative control, waiting through long timelines, and accepting lower royalties. If you want to focus on writing while letting a publisher handle logistics, this may be a good fit—just weigh the trade-offs carefully.

3. Align Publishing with Your Business Goals

Consider how each publishing path supports your overall objectives. For instance, if your book is a lead-generation tool, self-publishing allows you to include calls-to-action and links directly in your content. Traditional publishing might enhance credibility in certain industries but may limit your ability to use the book for direct marketing.

4. Budget for Publishing Costs

Whether you self-publish or go the traditional route, understand the costs involved. Self-publishing requires investment in editing, cover design, formatting, and marketing. Traditional publishing might cover these expenses but will take a larger share of royalties. Plan your budget carefully to ensure you're financially prepared for either option.

5. Test Audience Interest Before Committing

Share a sample chapter or concept with your target audience to gauge their interest. This can be done through social media, newsletters, or beta readers. Use the feedback to refine your book and confirm its appeal. This step not only validates your idea but also helps you decide which publishing method aligns with your audience's needs.

CHAPTER 7

Preparing Your Manuscript

Editing and Proofreading Tips

Editing and proofreading are crucial steps in getting your manuscript ready for publication. When I first started, I underestimated the importance of professional editing. I thought I could catch all the errors myself, but having a fresh set of eyes on your work is invaluable. Professional editors not only correct mistakes but also help improve the flow and clarity of your writing.

There are different types of editing. Developmental editing looks at the big picture, such as the structure of your book, the coherence of your arguments, and the development of your ideas. Copyediting focuses on the finer details like grammar, punctuation, and style. Proofreading is the final check for typos and minor errors before publication. Each type of editing plays a vital role in polishing your manuscript.

Self-editing is also important. Before sending your work to a professional, it helps to go through it yourself. I find it useful to read my manuscript aloud. This helps catch awkward phrasing and errors that you might miss when reading silently. Tools like Grammarly can assist with grammar and style, but they're no substitute for a thorough read-through by a human editor.

Formatting Your Book for Different Platforms

Once your manuscript is edited, the next step is formatting. This involves setting up your book so it looks good in print and digital formats. Print books and ebooks have different formatting requirements, so it's important to understand these differences.

For print, pay attention to margins, fonts, and layout. You want your book to be visually appealing and easy to read. Key elements include consistent chapter headings, page numbers, and a clean layout. Tools like Adobe InDesign and Microsoft Word can be helpful for formatting print books.

Ebooks, on the other hand, need to be flexible to accommodate various screen sizes and devices. This means avoiding complex layouts and ensuring your text flows smoothly. Kindle Create and Vellum are great tools for formatting ebooks. They help convert your manuscript into a format that works well on different ereaders.

Collaborating with Professional Editors

When I wrote my first book, I had no idea how much of a difference the right editor could make. I thought that because I had so much experience in the field, including in editing, another editor wouldn't make that big of a difference. I also knew my content was solid. However, I'm so glad I listened to everyone's advice: *Don't edit your own work.* Finding the right editor felt overwhelming at first, but it ended up being one of the best investments I made—not just in my book but in my business.

I started by asking other authors I trusted for recommendations and researching editors who understood my genre and audience. But here's what I learned: the magic happens when you find someone who doesn't just edit words but helps bring your vision to life. A great editor doesn't change your voice; they refine it, making your message clearer and more impactful.

When you work with an editor, sharing your vision is crucial. I sent mine a summary of my book, my goals, and the specific areas I was struggling with—like tightening up my storytelling and making sure the content flowed smoothly. This open communication helped them focus on what mattered most to me.

That's why our editing services are designed to do exactly that. We don't just proofread for grammar and typos; we partner with you to shape your book into a tool that works for your business. Whether it's refining your tone, organizing your content, or sharpening your message, our goal is to make sure your book connects with your audience and positions you as the authority you are.

Enhancing Your Book's Impact

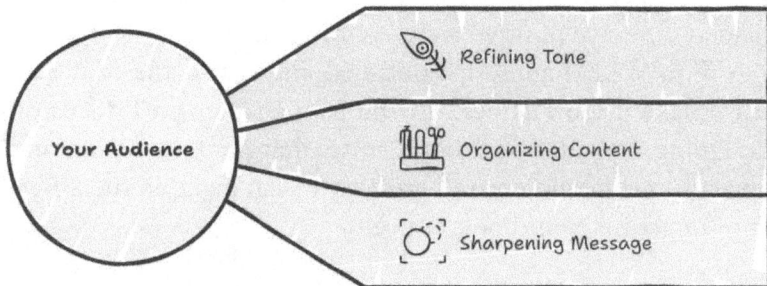

Managing feedback and revisions is a collaborative process. Regardless of who you work with, be open to suggestions, but also trust your instincts about what works best for your book. Sometimes, editors will make suggestions you might not agree with, and that's okay. It's your book, and you have the final say. However, it's important to consider their expertise and be willing to make changes that improve the overall quality of your manuscript.

Preparing your manuscript involves careful editing, proper formatting, and effective collaboration with professional editors. By taking the time to polish your work, you ensure your book is of the highest quality and ready for publication. These steps might seem tedious, but they are essential in creating a book that readers will enjoy and appreciate.

One of my clients, Emma, had completed her manuscript but was unsure about how to prepare it for publication. She knew the content was strong but felt overwhelmed by the editing and formatting process. I guided her through self-editing first, teaching her to read her work aloud to catch awkward phrasing and errors. Then, my editor helped her improve the flow and clarity of her writing while catching grammatical mistakes.

Once her manuscript was polished, we created a professionally designed book for her. As a result, Emma's book was well-edited and visually appealing, and she was proud of the final product. Her polished book helped her stand out in her field and receive positive reviews from readers.

With your manuscript polished and ready, the next step is to make it look its best. In the next chapter, we'll focus on designing a professional book cover that grabs attention and appeals to your audience. A great cover can make all the difference in getting your book noticed.

How to Prepare Your Manuscript for Success

1. Create a Detailed Outline Before You Write

A solid outline is the foundation of a successful manuscript. Begin by breaking your book into chapters, then identify the key points you'll cover in each. For instance, if your book is about personal finance, create sections like budgeting, investing, and saving. An outline keeps your writing focused and ensures your content flows logically.

2. Set Clear Writing Goals and Deadlines

Avoid the overwhelm of writing an entire manuscript by setting small, manageable goals. Aim to complete one chapter or 1,000 words each week. Set realistic deadlines and track your progress to stay motivated. For example, use a calendar or project management app to schedule writing sessions. Consistency ensures your manuscript stays on track.

3. Write with Your Audience in Mind

Tailor your language, tone, and examples to your target audience. For instance, if your readers are new entrepreneurs, keep your tone approachable and include examples relevant to small businesses. Avoid technical jargon unless you're writing for a specialized audience. Writing with your readers in mind makes your manuscript engaging and relatable.

4. Focus on Clarity Over Perfection

Don't let the fear of imperfection slow you down. Your first draft is a starting point, not the final product. Focus on getting your ideas on the page, knowing you'll refine them later. For example, write freely and return to polish your sentences during editing. Clear, focused writing is better than striving for flawless prose in the first draft.

5. Review and Revise Regularly

As you complete each section, take time to review and revise. Check for logical flow, clarity, and relevance. For example, ask yourself if the chapter's content aligns with your book's purpose. Revising as you go saves time and ensures your manuscript develops into a polished, cohesive book. Regular reviews help you identify and fix issues early.

CHAPTER 8

Designing a Professional Book Cover

Importance of a Strong Cover Design

When I started thinking about my book cover, I knew it had to be special. A strong cover design is crucial because it's the first thing potential readers see. It's like a storefront window that invites people to come in and explore. If the cover looks amateurish or doesn't catch the eye, people are likely to pass it by without a second thought. A well-designed cover can significantly impact sales and marketing. It helps your book stand out in a crowded marketplace, grabs attention, and piques curiosity.

An effective book cover needs to convey the essence of your book at a glance. It should be visually appealing, with a good balance of colors, fonts, and imagery. The title should be clear and readable, even at a thumbnail size, which is how most people will see it online. The cover should also hint at the genre and tone of your book, giving potential readers an idea of what to expect.

Anatomy of an Effective Book Cover

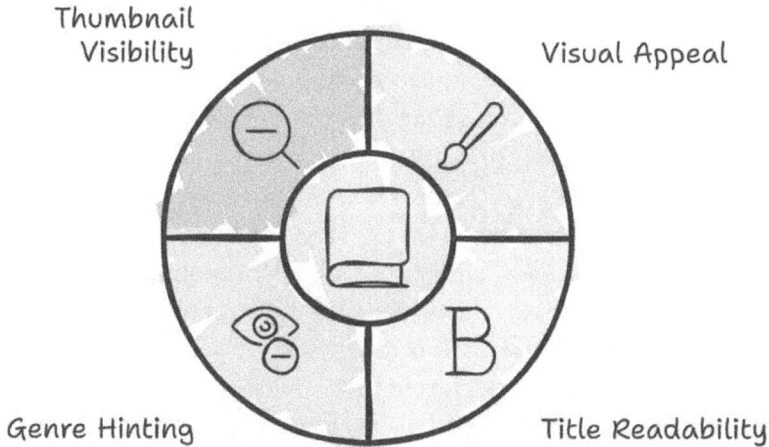

Thumbnail Visibility

Visual Appeal

Genre Hinting

Title Readability

Working with Designers

Communicating your vision to the designer is key. I provided a detailed brief that included a summary of my book, the themes I wanted to highlight, and any specific ideas I had for the cover. This helped ensure the designer had a clear understanding of what I was looking for. Throughout the process, I gave feedback and made sure we were on the same page. It's important to be open to the designer's suggestions, as they bring a professional eye to the project.

I looked at examples of successful book covers to understand what worked well. Covers that effectively use color, imagery, and typography to create a cohesive and striking design tend to perform best. For instance, a cover with a bold, readable title and a compelling image that relates to the book's content can draw readers in and make them want to know more.

DIY Book Cover Design

For those who prefer to design their own cover, there are plenty of tools and resources available. Software like Canva and Adobe Photoshop offer templates and design elements that can help you create a professional-looking cover. While designing your own cover can save money, it's important to invest time in learning basic design principles.

When creating a DIY cover, focus on simplicity and clarity. Choose a color scheme that reflects the mood of your book and select fonts that are easy to read. The graphics need to be high-quality and relevant to your book's content. Avoid overcrowding the cover with too much text or too many images, which can make it look cluttered.

There are common pitfalls to watch out for when designing your cover. One of the biggest is using low-resolution images, which can make the cover look unprofessional. It's also important to ensure the title and author name are readable in small sizes, as many people will see your cover as a thumbnail online. Finally, getting feedback from others can help catch any issues you might have missed.

Whether you work with a designer or do it yourself, designing a professional book cover is an essential part of preparing your book for publication. A strong cover can make a significant difference in attracting readers and making your book stand out. By focusing on the key elements of effective design and being mindful of common mistakes, you can create a great cover that helps your book succeed in the market.

Anna knew her book needed a standout cover but wasn't sure where to start. She wanted something that would reflect the themes of her book while grabbing attention online. My cover designer focused on making sure the cover communicated her book's message clearly and would stand out in a crowded marketplace.

We ensured the colors and imagery aligned with Anna's vision throughout the design process. The result was a bold, eye-catching cover with a clear, readable title that made her book look professional and engaging. After launching, the cover played a big role in attracting readers and boosting her sales.

With your book cover designed, it's time to focus on getting your book out into the world. In the next chapter, we'll explore publishing platforms and distribution options to help your book reach the widest possible audience. This is where your book starts making its way to readers everywhere.

How to Design a Professional Book Cover

1. Understand the Importance of a Strong Cover

Your book's cover is your first opportunity to make an impression on readers. It should grab attention and reflect the book's content. For example, a business book might use bold typography and clean lines, while a self-help book could feature soft colors and inviting imagery. A professional cover sets the tone and builds trust with your audience.

2. Hire a Professional Designer

Unless you're skilled in graphic design, it's best to hire a professional who specializes in book covers. Designers understand elements like font pairing, color balance, and composition. For instance, a designer can ensure your cover looks great in both print and digital formats. A polished, professional design can significantly increase your book's appeal and marketability.

3. Use Colors and Fonts That Reflect Your Genre

Each genre has its own visual language. For example, thrillers often use dark, moody colors and bold fonts, while romance novels might feature soft pastels and elegant script.

Research popular books in your genre to identify trends. Your designer can help you incorporate these elements while keeping your cover unique and aligned with your brand.

4. Ensure Your Title Is Readable at Any Size

Whether viewed on a bookshelf or as a thumbnail online, your title must be clear and legible. Avoid overly intricate fonts or low-contrast color combinations. For instance, white text on a light background may be hard to read in small sizes. Test your design in different formats to ensure it's eye-catching and easy to read.

5. Test Your Cover with Your Audience

Before finalizing your cover, gather feedback from your target audience. Share a few design options and ask which they prefer. For example, you can conduct a poll on social media or use a survey to gather insights. Testing ensures your cover resonates with readers and increases the likelihood they'll pick up your book.

CHAPTER 9

Publishing Platforms and Distribution

Choosing the Right Publishing Platforms

When it's time to choose a publishing platform for your book, you'll want to understand the options available. The two major self-publishing platforms to consider are Amazon KDP and IngramSpark. Amazon KDP is popular because it's straightforward and gives you access to Amazon's vast marketplace. It's easy to use and free to set up, though Amazon takes a cut of your sales. IngramSpark, on the other hand, offers wider distribution, including bookstores and libraries, but it has setup fees and can be a bit more complex to navigate.

Amazon KDP
Easy setup, direct access to Amazon marketplace

IngramSpark
Wider distribution, setup fees

In the end, selecting the best platform for your book depends on your goals and resources. You can also use both platforms. I published through Amazon KDP for the ease of reaching a large audience quickly and chose Expanded Distribution when publishing the paperback. Expanded Distribution simply means your book is listed in the Ingram catalog, which is the same service IngramSpark provides. Most bookstores order directly from the Ingram catalog, plus you'll be listed in 40,000 other book distribution sites, including Barnes & Noble, Books-A-Million, and Kobo. This combination allowed me to maximize my book's distribution and reach a broader audience.

Managing Your Ebook Version

While many people still prefer the feel of a paperback, others prefer the ease and portability of ebooks. How you format the ebook version is critical. How many times have you read an ebook that had a font size so large that a chapter title took up two to three pages or found other annoying design issues?

Also, ebooks are designed to flow and do not have pages like a print book. Think in terms of screens instead of pages. One chapter will cover many screens if you're reading an ebook on a small screen, like your phone. However, if you're reading the same chapter on your laptop, it might only cover a few screens.

By carefully choosing publishing platforms, setting up distribution channels, and managing both print and digital versions, I was able to ensure my book reached as many readers as possible in the formats they preferred and enjoyed reading. This comprehensive approach to publishing and distribution helped maximize my book's impact and sales.

One of my clients, Jon, was unsure which publishing platform to choose for his book. He wanted it to be available on Amazon but also wanted to reach bookstores and libraries. I helped him decide on a dual approach, using Amazon KDP for its ease and access to Amazon's massive audience while also setting up his book on IngramSpark for wider distribution.

We used Amazon KDP for the ebook and paperback versions, enabling Expanded Distribution to list the book in Ingram's catalog. For bookstores and libraries, we published through IngramSpark. This strategy gave John the best of both worlds: quick access to Amazon's marketplace and broader exposure to bookstores and libraries. As a result, his book reached a wide audience, and his sales saw a significant boost from both online and offline channels.

Now that you know how to distribute your book, it's time to talk about pricing it right. The next chapter will explore strategies for setting the perfect price and understanding royalties. This will help you balance making your book accessible while ensuring it supports your business goals.

How to Choose Publishing Platforms and Distribute Your Book

1. Understand the Differences Between Platforms

Publishing platforms vary in features, royalties, and distribution options. For example, Amazon KDP offers global reach for both ebooks and paperbacks, while IngramSpark provides access to bookstores and libraries. Research each platform to determine which aligns with your goals. Understanding these differences helps you choose the best fit for your book.

2. Decide Between Print, Digital, or Both

Determine whether you'll publish your book as an ebook, a paperback, or both. For instance, ebooks are cost-effective and accessible worldwide, while print books offer a tangible experience that many readers prefer. Consider your audience's preferences and how each format aligns with your publishing goals. Offering both options can maximize your reach.

3. Evaluate Royalties and Costs

Each platform has its own pricing model and royalty structure. For example, Amazon KDP typically offers a 70 percent royalty rate for ebooks priced between $2.99 and $9.99, while print books have additional printing costs. Compare the costs and potential earnings of each platform to ensure profitability. Transparent budgeting helps you avoid surprises later.

4. Research Distribution Options

Some platforms, like IngramSpark, allow you to distribute your book to retailers and libraries, while Amazon primarily focuses on its own ecosystem. Decide where you want your book to be available. For example, if your goal is to get your book into local bookstores, prioritize a platform with broader distribution channels. Strategic distribution ensures your book reaches the right audience.

5. Test the Publishing Process

Before officially launching, test the publishing process by creating a draft version of your book. For instance, upload a sample file to ensure formatting looks correct on all devices. Use print proofs to check for quality and design accuracy. Testing helps you catch potential issues and ensures your book meets professional standards.

CHAPTER 10

Pricing and Royalties

Strategies for Pricing Your Book

When I started thinking about pricing my book, I quickly realized that setting the right price is more of an art than a science. Several factors came into play, such as my goals for the book, my target audience, and the production costs. I had to find a balance between making my book affordable and covering the financial and time investments.

One of the first things I did was conduct a competitive pricing analysis. I looked at other books in my genre to see what similar titles were selling for. This gave me a good benchmark from which to work. If my book was priced too high compared to others, potential readers might skip it. On the other hand, pricing it too low could make it seem like it wasn't valuable.

Psychological pricing techniques also came into play. For instance, pricing a book at $9.99 instead of $10.00 can make it seem like a better deal, even though the difference is just a penny. This small tweak can significantly affect how people perceive the price. I also considered offering my book at a lower price when it first launched to attract early buyers and generate initial reviews, which are crucial for long-term sales.

Understanding Royalties and Payments

Understanding how royalties work was another crucial aspect. In self-publishing, platforms like Amazon KDP and IngramSpark offer different royalty rates depending on the book's price and format (print or digital). With Amazon KDP, for example, I could choose between a 35 percent or 70 percent royalty rate for ebooks, depending on the price I set. Knowing these rates helped me calculate my potential earnings more accurately.

In traditional publishing, the process is different. Publishers typically offer an advance against royalties, which is a lump sum paid upfront. Once the book starts selling, royalties are paid out, but only after the advance has been "earned back" by the publisher. This means the author doesn't receive additional royalty payments until enough books have been sold to cover the advance.

For self-published books, tracking and managing royalty payments can be a bit of a challenge. Most platforms provide detailed sales reports, but it's important to keep your own records as well. I made a habit of regularly checking my sales and tracking the payments to ensure everything matched up. This helped me stay on top of my finances and make informed decisions about future pricing and marketing strategies.

Special Pricing Strategies

Special pricing strategies can also play a significant role in a book's success. Offering limited-time discounts and promotions is one way to boost sales. For example, I ran a discounted price for the first week of my book's release to generate buzz and encourage more people to buy it right away. This initial surge in sales helped improve my book's ranking on Amazon, making it more visible to potential readers.

Setting the right price for your book involves understanding your market, using psychological pricing techniques, and considering your costs. Understanding how royalties work and keeping track of your earnings is crucial for managing your finances. Special pricing strategies like discounts, bundles, and subscriptions can help boost your sales and build a loyal audience. By carefully planning your pricing and royalty strategies, you can maximize your book's potential and achieve your financial goals.

Book Pricing and Royalty Strategies

Market Understanding

Knowing your market helps set competitive prices and target the right audience.

Psychological Pricing

Using psychological pricing can influence buyer perception and increase sales.

Cost Consideration

Considering costs ensures profitability and sustainable pricing.

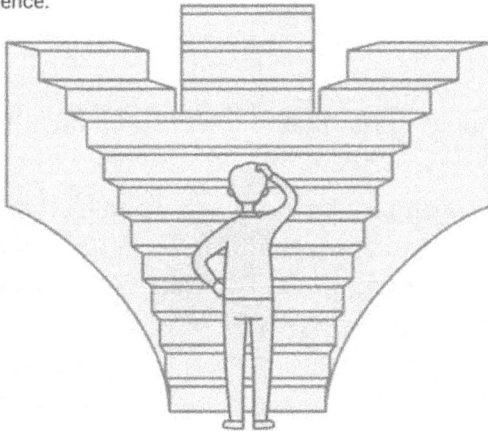

Lisa was unsure how to price her self-published book. She wanted to strike a balance between affordability and making sure her book appeared valuable to her target audience.

First, we conducted a competitive analysis by looking at similar books in her genre and identifying a pricing sweet spot. Together, we decided on 99¢ for her ebook and $9.99 for her print book, aiming to get more sales rather than trying to make an extra dollar or two in royalties.

We also discussed running a special launch-week discount to generate early sales and reviews, which helped boost her book's ranking on Amazon. By tracking her sales and adjusting the price as needed, Lisa hit her sales goals and established a solid reader base early on. This thoughtful approach to pricing and royalties helped her maximize her book's potential and create a long-term revenue stream for her business.

With your book's pricing and royalties in place, it's time to focus on the next big step: launching your book and building your book funnel. In the next section, we'll explore how to create a successful book launch that grabs attention and sets up a system to guide readers into your funnel, turning them into loyal customers.

How to Set Pricing and Understand Royalties

1. Research Comparable Books in Your Genre

Look at the pricing of similar books in your genre to establish a competitive price. For instance, if business books typically range from $9.99 to $19.99, choose a price within that range. Analyze the value and content length of your book compared to others to ensure your pricing aligns with reader expectations.

2. Understand How Royalties Work

Familiarize yourself with the royalty structures of different platforms. For example, Amazon KDP offers a 70 percent royalty for ebooks priced between $2.99 and $9.99 but drops to 35 percent outside this range. Platforms like IngramSpark have varying royalty rates depending on distribution. Knowing the details helps you make informed pricing decisions.

3. Factor in Production Costs for Print Books

For print books, consider printing costs when setting your price. Platforms like Amazon KDP and IngramSpark charge for printing based on page count and format. For example, a 200-page book might cost $3 to print. Ensure your retail price covers these costs while leaving room for profit and competitive pricing.

4. Balance Affordability with Perceived Value

Price your book to be both accessible to readers and reflective of its value. For instance, a high-quality, in-depth book on a specialized topic can justify a higher price. However, if your book is shorter or introductory, consider a lower price to attract a broader audience. Perceived value influences purchasing decisions.

5. Test and Adjust Your Pricing

Experiment with different price points to see what resonates with your audience. For example, run promotions or limited-time discounts to gauge response. Track sales data to identify trends, such as increased purchases at certain price points. Testing helps you find the sweet spot that maximizes both sales and revenue.

SECTION 3

Book Launch 2.0

In this section, you'll discover how to turn your book into a tool that brings in new customers and grows your business. Each step helps you create a system—a book funnel—that turns readers into clients. By following this process, your book won't just sit on a shelf; it will work for you.

Clarity is all about making sure your book's message is clear and connects directly to your business. When your book has a strong, focused message, it's easier for readers to understand how you can help them.

Congruency ensures everything in your book matches your business and brand. This creates a smooth and natural connection between what readers learn from your book and what your business offers.

Conversion shows you how to include simple, smart ways to encourage readers to take action, like visiting your website or signing up for more information. This step turns readers into potential customers.

Capture is about gathering your readers' contact information so you can stay in touch. Building this connection is important for creating relationships that lead to business opportunities.

Campaign helps you promote your book and share it with a wider audience. This step includes tips for running marketing campaigns and getting your book in front of the right people.

Finally, **Catalyst** shows you how to use your book as a key part of your overall marketing strategy. With the right approach, your book can be the spark that grows your business in exciting ways.

Each of these steps works together to create a funnel that brings people closer to your business. This section will teach you how to make your book a powerful tool for attracting, connecting with, and converting readers into loyal clients.

The first step in creating an effective book funnel is achieving clarity. In the next chapter, we'll explore how to ensure your book's message is clear, focused, and directly connected to your business goals. Clarity is the foundation that makes your funnel work.

Book Launch 2.0

Use your book to attract clients

Clarity

Ensure your book's message is clear and aligned with your business, helping readers understand how you can assist them.

Conversion

Implement strategies to encourage action, like visiting your website, turning readers into potential customers.

Congruency

Align your book's content with your brand, ensuring a seamless connection between the book and your business offerings.

Capture

Gather reader contact details to build relationships and create business opportunities through continuous engagement.

Catalyst

Use your book strategically as part of your marketing plan to ignite business growth.

Campaign

Promote your book effectively to reach a wider audience, with strategic marketing campaigns.

CHAPTER 11

Clarity

Identifying Client Pain Points

When I first sat down to write my book, I knew I needed to understand my readers deeply. Specifically, I had to get a clear picture of their struggles and challenges. Knowing their pain points is crucial because it allows you to address their needs directly and offer real solutions.

I started by thinking about my ideal clients. These are the people who would benefit most from my book. I asked myself what keeps them up at night. What obstacles are they facing that my book could help them overcome? To get these answers, I did some research. I looked at forums and social media groups and read reviews of similar books. This gave me insight into common problems and concerns.

Another technique I found useful was talking to my existing clients. I asked them about their biggest challenges and what solutions they were seeking. These conversations were invaluable because they provided real-world examples and allowed me to empathize with my readers' struggles. By understanding their pain points, I could tailor my content to address their specific needs and make my book more relevant and useful.

Identifying Ideal Clients for a Book

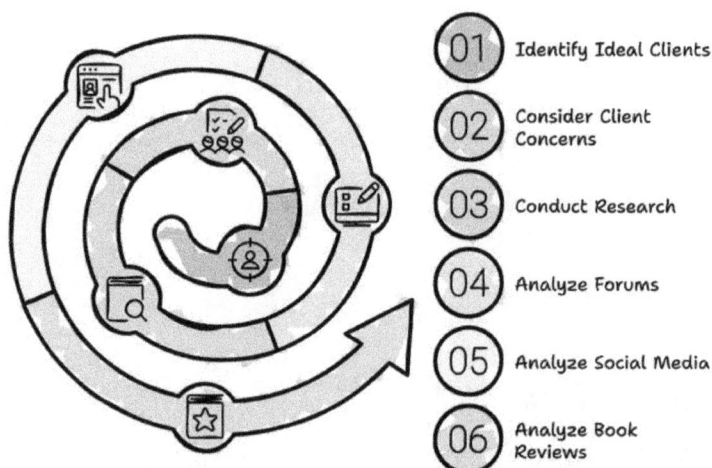

01 Identify Ideal Clients

02 Consider Client Concerns

03 Conduct Research

04 Analyze Forums

05 Analyze Social Media

06 Analyze Book Reviews

Envisioning the Solution

Once I clearly understood my readers' pain points, the next step was to envision the solution. This means imagining what my ideal client's life would look like after their problem is solved. It's important to create a vision that aligns with my book's message and offers hope and inspiration.

I pictured a reader who had implemented the strategies from my book and was now experiencing positive changes. Maybe they were more confident, had increased their business revenue, or felt less stressed and more in control. Describing this transformation in my book helped create a compelling vision that readers could aspire to.

Crafting this vision was about more than just listing benefits. It was about telling a story that connected emotionally with my readers. I wanted them to see themselves in the success stories I shared and feel motivated to take action. By aligning this vision with my book's value proposition, I made sure my content was informative and inspiring.

Writing with clarity about both the problems my readers face and the solutions my book offers made my message stronger. It showed that I understood their struggles and had a clear plan to help them achieve their goals. This approach made my book more engaging and built trust with my readers, as they could see that I genuinely cared about helping them succeed.

One of my clients, Mike, was writing a book to help small business owners overcome financial challenges. He struggled with identifying his readers' key pain points. I helped him by guiding him through research, including looking at online forums, social media, and reviews of similar books. We also talked to his existing clients to gather real-world examples of their struggles with managing cash flow.

Once Mike clearly understood his readers' pain points, we worked on envisioning the solutions his book would offer. Together, we crafted a vision of success—small business owners feeling more in control of their finances, growing their revenue, and reducing stress. This vision made Mike's book more relatable and gave his readers hope that his strategies could truly make a difference. By writing with this clarity, Mike deeply connected with his audience and built trust, making his book more impactful.

Now that you've established clarity, congruency is the next step in creating an effective book funnel. In the next chapter, we'll explore how to align your book's content, tone, and design with your brand and business goals. This alignment ensures a seamless experience that keeps readers engaged and moving through your funnel.

How to Set Pricing and Understand Royalties

1. Research Comparable Books in Your Genre

Look at the pricing of similar books in your genre to establish a competitive price. For instance, if business books typically range from $9.99 to $19.99, choose a price within that range. Analyze the value and content length of your book compared to others to ensure your pricing aligns with reader expectations.

2. Understand How Royalties Work

Familiarize yourself with the royalty structures of different platforms. For example, Amazon KDP offers a 70 percent royalty for ebooks priced between $2.99 and $9.99 but drops to 35 percent outside this range. Platforms like IngramSpark have varying royalty rates depending on distribution. Knowing the details helps you make informed pricing decisions.

3. Factor in Production Costs for Print Books

For print books, consider printing costs when setting your price. Platforms like Amazon KDP and IngramSpark charge for printing based on page count and format. For example, a 200-page book might cost $3 to print. Ensure your retail price covers these costs while leaving room for profit and competitive pricing.

4. Balance Affordability with Perceived Value

Price your book to be both accessible to readers and reflective of its value. For instance, a high-quality, in-depth book on a specialized topic can justify a higher price. However, if your book is shorter or introductory, consider a lower price to attract a broader audience. Perceived value influences purchasing decisions.

5. Test and Adjust Your Pricing

Experiment with different price points to see what resonates with your audience. For example, run promotions or limited-time discounts to gauge response. Track sales data to identify trends, such as increased purchases at certain price points. Testing helps you find the sweet spot that maximizes both sales and revenue.

CHAPTER 12

Congruency

Aligning Your Book and Brand

When I began writing my book, I knew it needed to be more than just a collection of my thoughts and advice; it had to reflect my brand's values and voice. This alignment was crucial because I wanted my book to be a true extension of my business. If someone picked up my book, they should get the same feeling and message they would get from interacting with my business in any other way.

To ensure this alignment, I started by clearly defining what my brand stands for. My brand values honesty, practical advice, and a touch of humor. I made sure that these elements came through in my writing. For instance, if my brand's voice is casual and friendly, my book needed to match that tone. This consistency helps build a strong brand identity and makes my book an effective marketing tool.

Integrating the book into my overall marketing strategy was the next step. I thought about how the book could support and enhance my other marketing efforts. For example, I used the book to drive traffic to my website by including links and references to additional resources. I also aligned my book launch with my marketing campaigns, using the same themes and messages to create a cohesive experience for my audience. This strategic integration ensured my book wasn't just an isolated project but a key part of my marketing toolkit.

Integrating Book into Marketing Strategy

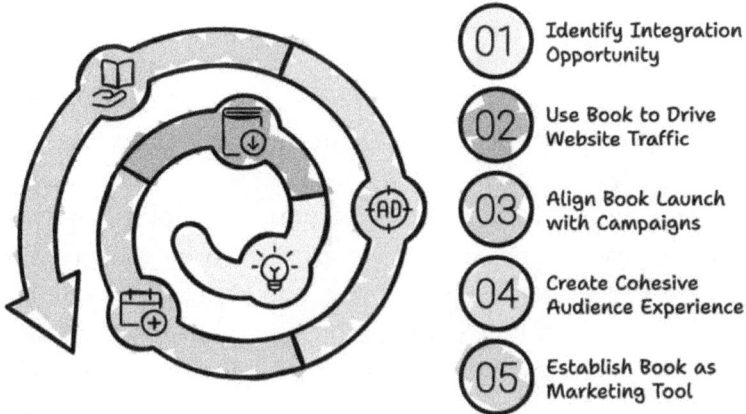

01 Identify Integration Opportunity

02 Use Book to Drive Website Traffic

03 Align Book Launch with Campaigns

04 Create Cohesive Audience Experience

05 Establish Book as Marketing Tool

Using Consistent Messaging

Maintaining consistent language and tone across all platforms is essential for a strong brand presence. I made sure that the message of my book was consistent with what I communicated on my website, social media, and other marketing materials. This consistency helps reinforce my brand and makes it easier for people to recognize and trust my message.

One technique I used was creating a style guide for my book and other content. This guide included guidelines on tone, word choice, and formatting. Having this reference ensured everything I produced had a similar feel and voice. It also made it easier to delegate tasks to others, knowing they had clear guidelines to follow.

There are many examples of successful marketing campaigns where congruency plays a key role. Take Apple, for instance. Every piece of their marketing, from their sleek website to their minimalist product packaging, reflects their brand's values of innovation and simplicity. This consistent messaging helps build a strong, recognizable brand.

I created a cohesive and effective marketing tool by aligning my book with my brand and maintaining consistent messaging across all platforms. My book became more than just a source of information; it was a powerful extension of my brand that helped to reinforce my message and build trust with my audience.

One of my clients, Karen, was writing a book to complement her coaching business. She wanted the book to reflect her brand's core values of empowerment, authenticity, and simplicity but struggled to keep her tone consistent. I helped her define her brand's voice by reviewing her existing content—her website, social media, and email newsletters—and ensuring the same friendly, supportive tone was present throughout her book.

We created a style guide for her writing, which included guidelines on word choice, tone, and formatting. This helped her stay aligned with her brand as she wrote, and it made it easier to incorporate the book into her overall marketing strategy. By ensuring her book had the same message and tone as the rest of her business, Karen's readers felt a seamless connection between the book and her brand. This congruency boosted trust and helped convert readers into clients for her coaching services.

With congruency in place, it's time to focus on conversion—the key to turning readers into leads. In the next chapter, we'll discuss how to create compelling calls-to-action and strategies that encourage readers to take the next step. This is where your book starts working as a powerful tool in your funnel.

How to Ensure Congruency Between Your Book and Brand

1. Match Your Tone to Your Brand Voice

Your book's tone should reflect your brand identity. If your brand is professional and authoritative, maintain that tone throughout. Alternatively, if your brand is conversational and approachable, write in a casual, friendly style. Consistency between your brand and book builds trust with readers and reinforces the authenticity of your overall message.

2. Align Visual Elements with Your Branding

Ensure your book's cover, colors, and typography align with your brand's visual identity. For example, if your website uses clean, minimalist designs, your book's design should reflect the same aesthetic. This visual congruence creates a seamless experience for your audience and strengthens the connection between your book and other brand assets.

3. Reinforce Your Core Message Throughout

Every chapter should tie back to your brand's central message or values. For instance, if your brand promotes sustainability, your book should emphasize eco-conscious examples and solutions. Consistently reinforcing your message ensures readers associate your book with your brand's mission, deepening their understanding and loyalty.

4. Include Brand-Specific CTAs

Add calls-to-action (CTAs) that direct readers to engage further with your brand. For example, encourage readers to visit your website, follow your social media accounts, or subscribe to your newsletter. Ensure these CTAs use your brand's language and tone, maintaining alignment with your broader marketing strategy.

5. Test for Congruency with Your Audience

Share drafts or design concepts with a sample of your audience to ensure your book aligns with their perception of your brand. Ask questions like, "Does this content feel consistent with my brand?" and "Does this design match what you expect from me?" Audience feedback helps fine-tune congruency and ensures your book meets expectations.

CHAPTER 13

Conversion

Designing Effective CTAs

When I set out to write my book, I knew that simply providing information wasn't enough. I needed to guide my readers to take action, which is where calls-to-action (CTAs) come into play. A compelling CTA encourages readers to engage further with your content, whether that's signing up for a newsletter, purchasing a product, or contacting you for services.

Creating an effective CTA involves several key elements. First, clarity is crucial. Your CTA should be straightforward, telling readers exactly what you want them to do. Phrases like "Sign Up Now" or "Get Your Free Guide" leave no room for confusion. The language should be active and direct, prompting immediate action.

Placement and timing also play a significant role in the effectiveness of CTAs. I found that placing CTAs at strategic points in the book, such as at the end of a chapter or after a particularly compelling section, worked best. This is when the reader is most engaged and likely to act. Additionally, repeating CTAs throughout the book can reinforce the message without being too pushy. For instance, a subtle reminder at the end of each chapter can encourage readers to visit your website or sign up for more information.

Optimizing Landing Pages

Once you've designed effective CTAs, the next step is to ensure the landing pages they direct to are optimized for conversion. A high-converting landing page is one that successfully turns visitors into leads or customers.

The key components of a successful landing page start with a clear, concise headline that immediately communicates the value of what you're offering. The headline should grab attention and make it clear why the visitor should care. Supporting this headline with compelling copy that highlights the benefits and features of your offer is essential.

Another critical element is social proof. Including testimonials from satisfied customers or endorsements from credible sources can significantly increase trust and credibility. When potential clients see that others have benefited from your product or service, they're more likely to believe they will, too. In my experience, adding a few well-placed testimonials can make a big difference in conversion rates.

Visuals are also important. High-quality images or videos can help illustrate your points and make the landing page more engaging. However, remember to keep the design clean and uncluttered. Too many elements can distract from the main message and overwhelm visitors.

A strong, visible CTA on the landing page is a must. This button should stand out and be easy to find, with action-oriented text that reinforces what the visitor will gain by clicking. Also, making the process as frictionless as possible is crucial. If you're asking visitors to fill out a form, keep it short and only request essential information. The easier you make it for them to take action, the more likely they are to convert.

Optimizing Landing Page Conversion

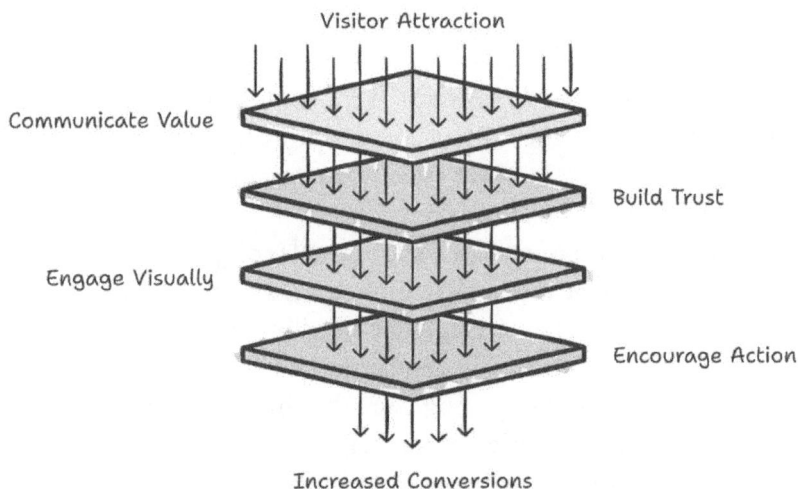

Visitor Attraction

Communicate Value

Build Trust

Engage Visually

Encourage Action

Increased Conversions

By focusing on clear, compelling CTAs and optimizing landing pages for conversion, I created a seamless path for readers to follow from my book to my broader business offerings. This enhanced the value of my book and helped grow my audience and client base.

Becky was using her book to attract clients for her coaching business. She had great content but wasn't sure how to guide her readers to take the next step. My team designed clear and compelling calls-to-action (CTAs) for her book, including the visual ad to go inside her book, along with a strong and compelling headline. We placed these CTAs at key points in the book, like at the end of each chapter, where readers were most engaged.

Next, I worked with Becky to optimize her landing pages. We created a simple but engaging headline that focused on the value she offered, added testimonials from satisfied clients, and included a prominent CTA button that stood out. She saw a significant boost in conversions by keeping the forms short and easy to complete, with more readers booking consultations and signing up for her services. This strategy enhanced the book's effectiveness and helped her grow her business.

Now that you've set up your book to convert readers into leads, the next step is to capture their information. In the next chapter, we'll explore strategies to collect and manage reader details effectively so you can build lasting connections. Capturing this information is crucial for nurturing relationships and guiding readers further through your funnel.

How to Convert Readers into Leads with Smart CTAs

1. Strategically Place CTAs Throughout the Book

Position CTAs at natural transition points, such as the end of chapters, to avoid disrupting the reader's experience. For example, after explaining a concept, include a CTA like, "Visit [YourWebsite.com] to download a free checklist." Thoughtful placement ensures readers notice your CTAs without feeling overwhelmed or distracted from the main content.

2. Offer High-Value Incentives

Provide readers with free resources that extend the value of your book, such as templates, guides, or video tutorials. For example, a book about productivity could offer a free daily planner template. High-value incentives encourage readers to engage with your brand and provide their contact information, turning them into potential leads.

3. Use Clear and Direct Language in CTAs

Avoid vague or passive phrasing in your CTAs. Instead, use action-oriented language like, "Click here to access exclusive resources." For instance, a book on marketing could direct readers to, "Sign up for our free webinar on social media strategies." Clear instructions make it easy for readers to act, increasing engagement rates.

4. Link CTAs to Tangible Benefits

Show readers the specific value they'll gain by following your CTA. For example, instead of saying, "Download my guide," explain, "Download this guide to learn five proven techniques for increasing sales." Highlighting benefits motivates readers to take action because they understand the immediate relevance of your offer to their needs.

5. Track and Analyze CTA Effectiveness

Use analytics tools to monitor how readers respond to your CTAs. For example, track how many people sign up for your email list after visiting a linked landing page. Reviewing this data helps you identify which CTAs perform best and refine your strategy to maximize lead conversion.

CHAPTER 14

Capture

Creating Irresistible Lead Magnets

When I began thinking about how to capture leads from my book, I realized the importance of creating something that would entice readers to provide their contact information. This is where lead magnets come into play. Lead magnets are valuable resources offered for free in exchange for a reader's email address or other contact details.

To craft an irresistible lead magnet, I started by considering what would be most beneficial to my audience. Since my readers were interested in growing their businesses through writing and publishing, I focused on creating content that provided immediate value and actionable insights. I offered a free ebook with step-by-step guides, templates, and checklists that complemented the material in my book. This added layer of value attracted more leads and enhanced the overall experience for my readers.

The key to an effective lead magnet is ensuring it delivers real value. It should solve a specific problem or answer a pressing question your audience has. I made sure my lead magnet was not just a teaser but a comprehensive resource that would leave readers feeling they had gained something substantial.

This approach builds trust and positions you as an authority in your field.

Lead Magnet Success Pyramid

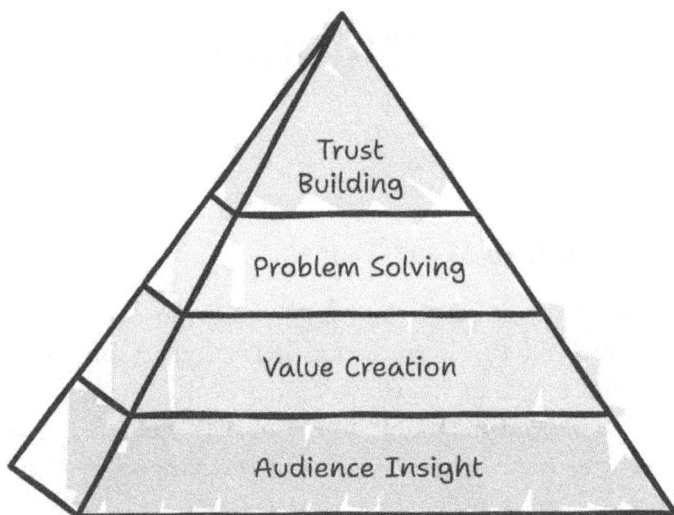

Promoting Opt-in Pages

Once I had my lead magnet, the next step was to promote it effectively. An opt-in page is where you capture the contact information of your leads. To drive traffic to these pages, I used a variety of strategies.

Social media was one of my primary tools for promotion. I shared posts that highlighted the benefits of my lead magnet and included direct links to the opt-in page. By using engaging visuals and compelling copy, I caught the attention of my followers and encouraged them to click through. Running targeted ads on platforms like Facebook and Instagram also helped me reach a broader audience beyond my immediate followers.

Email marketing was another effective strategy. I sent out newsletters to my existing email list, offering the lead magnet as a free gift. This not only helped capture new leads but also re-engaged my current subscribers by providing them with additional value.

Cross-promotion with other authors and influencers in my field also played a crucial role. I partnered with others who had a similar target audience and offered to share their content in exchange for them sharing mine. This mutual promotion helped expand my reach and brought in leads from new sources.

By creating a lead magnet that provided genuine value and using strategic promotion techniques, I captured a significant number of leads from my book. This process helped grow my email list and strengthened my relationship with my audience, setting the stage for future engagement and conversion.

My client Sarah's book was packed with valuable insights, but her readers weren't becoming clients. The problem? They didn't know how to apply what they'd learned, especially when it came to creating effective social media strategies—a major pain point in her industry.

To fix this, we created a lead magnet that filled the gap. This free guide included actionable templates and a seven-day content calendar, solving her readers' biggest struggle—knowing what to post to grow their businesses. A QR code embedded in her book made it easy to access.

We promoted the guide through a high-converting landing page, targeted ads, and strategic social media posts. Instead of just offering the blueprint, Sarah shared real-world results from clients who had implemented her strategies. This approach built trust and positioned her as the go-to authority.

The result? Sarah's email list grew rapidly, and her readers began reaching out for her paid services. By addressing a specific pain point, she turned her book into a springboard for deeper engagement and business growth.

With your system in place to capture reader information, it's time to launch your campaign. In the next chapter, we'll dive into strategies for promoting your book and funnel to a wider audience. A strong campaign will amplify your reach and ensure your book drives consistent growth for your business.

How to Capture Reader Information for Long-Term Engagement

1. Create a Dedicated Landing Page for Your Book

Build a landing page that offers exclusive content, like bonus chapters or tools, in exchange for email addresses. For instance, "Visit [YourWebsite.com/Resources] to download free templates from the book." A dedicated page makes it easy for readers to take the next step and ensures you can capture their contact information effectively.

2. Encourage Email Sign-Ups Within the Book

Place multiple prompts throughout your book inviting readers to join your email list. For example, "Want more tips like these? Subscribe at [YourWebsite.com] for weekly insights." Repeat these prompts at key points, such as after impactful sections, ensuring readers see them without feeling overwhelmed by constant reminders.

3. Incorporate Social Media CTAs

Direct readers to follow your social media profiles for ongoing engagement. For example, include a note like, "For daily tips, follow me on Instagram at @YourHandle." Social media extends your relationship with readers beyond the book, keeping them connected to your brand and encouraging interaction in different formats.

4. Use QR Codes for Convenience

Add QR codes in your book to simplify reader actions. For instance, place a QR code at the end of a chapter that links to additional resources or a sign-up page. This makes it easy for readers to access your content immediately, boosting engagement and increasing the likelihood they'll provide their information.

5. Provide Long-Term Value Through Follow-Ups

Develop a follow-up strategy, such as a series of emails or downloadable content, that continues to offer value. For instance, "Sign up for our newsletter and receive exclusive weekly tips on improving productivity." Long-term value builds trust and ensures readers remain engaged with your brand over time.

CHAPTER 15

Campaign

Planning Your Launch Campaign

When I decided to launch my book, I knew that a well-planned campaign would be crucial to its success. I started by setting clear goals for the campaign. I wanted to reach a specific number of sales within the first week, gain a certain number of reviews, and generate buzz around the release. Having these goals helped me focus my efforts and measure my progress.

Next, I created a timeline. I mapped out all the tasks that needed to be completed before the launch day and assigned deadlines to each. This included everything from finalizing the book cover to scheduling social media posts. Breaking down the process into manageable steps made it less overwhelming and ensured nothing was overlooked.

Creating a detailed launch plan was my next step. This plan served as a roadmap, guiding me through the entire process. It included strategies for building anticipation, such as sneak peeks and countdowns, as well as outreach efforts, like contacting bloggers and influencers for reviews and interviews. I could ensure a smooth and organized launch by planning these activities in advance.

Set Campaign Goals	Create Timeline	Develop Launch Plan
Establishing clear objectives for sales and reviews	Organizing tasks with deadlines for launch preparation	Outlining strategies for anticipation and outreach

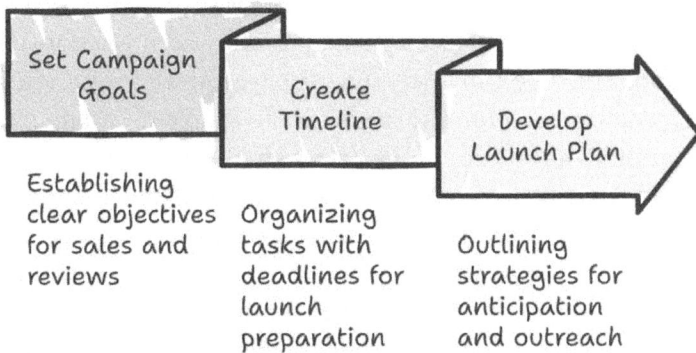

Executing Launch Day Strategies

When the launch day arrived, I knew I had to coordinate several activities to make it a success. I started the day by emailing my subscribers, announcing that the book was now available. I also posted on all my social media channels, sharing links to where the book could be purchased and encouraging my followers to share the news.

One of the key strategies was to create a sense of urgency. I offered limited-time discounts and bonuses for those who bought the book on launch day. This not only boosted sales but also helped generate excitement and word-of-mouth promotion. I monitored sales and engagement throughout the day, promptly responding to comments and questions.

Post-launch follow-up was just as important as the activities on the launch day itself. In the days following the release, I continued to engage with my audience. I thanked those who purchased the book and encouraged them to leave reviews. Positive reviews are essential for building credibility and attracting new readers. I also contacted those who had expressed interest but hadn't yet made a purchase, offering reminders and additional incentives.

Keeping the momentum going was key. I scheduled follow-up emails and social media posts to keep the conversation about the book alive. By staying engaged with my audience and continuing to promote the book, I was able to sustain interest and drive more sales in the weeks after the launch.

Planning and executing a successful launch campaign involves setting clear goals, creating a detailed plan, and coordinating activities effectively. By focusing on both the launch day and the days that followed, I ensured my book received the attention it deserved and reached as many readers as possible. This approach helped me achieve my sales targets and laid the foundation for long-term success.

Bryan was launching his first book and wanted to ensure his campaign succeeded. Together, we set clear goals for his launch, including reaching a target number of sales and reviews within the first week. We then created a detailed timeline, breaking down all the tasks he needed to complete leading up to the launch, like finalizing his cover, scheduling posts, and reaching out to influencers for early reviews.

On launch day, Bryan followed our plan, sending emails to his subscribers and posting across his social media platforms. We also implemented a limited-time discount to create urgency, which helped drive sales and generate buzz. After the launch, Bryan stayed engaged with his audience, thanking buyers and encouraging reviews. By following this structured campaign, he surpassed his sales targets, generated plenty of positive reviews, and kept the momentum going long after launch day, ensuring his book's continued success.

Now that your campaign is up and running, it's time to focus on the final step: making your book the catalyst for long-term success. In the next chapter, we'll explore how to use your book as the centerpiece of your marketing strategy, driving growth and creating new opportunities for your business. This is where your book becomes a game-changer.

How to Plan and Execute a Successful Book Campaign

1. Define Clear Campaign Objectives

Determine what you want to achieve with your book campaign. For example, your goals might include selling 1,000 copies, growing your email list by 500 subscribers, or booking five speaking engagements. Clear objectives guide your strategy and ensure your efforts are focused on achieving measurable results.

2. Build Buzz Before the Launch

Start promoting your book several weeks before its release. Share sneak peeks, host giveaways, and create countdown posts on social media. For example, offer free chapters to subscribers or exclusive bonuses for pre-orders. Pre-launch buzz builds anticipation and ensures your audience is ready to act when your book is available.

3. Leverage Multiple Marketing Channels

Use a combination of email marketing, social media, podcast interviews, and paid ads to reach your audience. For instance, run Facebook ads targeting readers of similar books and pitch yourself as a guest on industry podcasts. Diversifying your channels increases your book's visibility and ensures a broader reach.

4. Engage Your Network for Support

Ask colleagues, friends, and influencers to share your book with their audiences. For example, send personalized messages asking them to review or promote your book. Offering a free copy in exchange for honest feedback can also encourage participation. Leveraging your network expands your reach and boosts credibility.

5. Monitor and Optimize Your Efforts

Track key metrics like sales, engagement rates, and website traffic throughout your campaign. For instance, use Google Analytics to see which ads or posts drive the most clicks. Use this data to refine your strategy, focusing on what works best to maximize results for your book campaign.

CHAPTER 16

Catalyst

Leveraging Your Book for Business Growth

Writing a book can be a game-changer for your business. When I first published my book, I didn't fully grasp just how powerful it could be. Almost immediately, I saw a shift. My book became a calling card, something tangible that demonstrated my expertise and commitment to my field. It opened doors I hadn't even considered before.

Having a book establishes you as an authority in your industry. People start to see you as a credible source of knowledge, which can significantly boost your reputation. This credibility leads to more opportunities. For example, I was invited to speak at conferences and participate in panel discussions. These appearances broadened my reach and allowed me to connect with other experts and potential clients.

The impact on my business was profound. Clients who read my book felt they knew me before we even met. This pre-established trust made our interactions smoother and more productive. The book also provided a passive income stream, which supplemented my primary business activities. It acted as a constant advertisement, continually drawing in new clients and opportunities long after the initial launch.

Many entrepreneurs have leveraged their books to achieve remarkable success. Take Barbara Corcoran, for example. Her book *Shark Tales* shared her journey from a struggling real estate agent to a business mogul and solidified her reputation as an authority in entrepreneurship. The book opened doors to media appearances, speaking engagements, and, ultimately, her role as a judge on *Shark Tank*.

Similarly, my book became a cornerstone of my brand, driving new opportunities, expanding my reach, and positioning me as a trusted expert in my field. Like Barbara, I used my story and expertise to build a platform that elevated my business to the next level.

Expanding Your Reach

One of the most exciting aspects of publishing a book is the way it expands your reach. I found that my book opened doors to public speaking and media coverage that I hadn't anticipated. Speaking engagements are a powerful way to share your message with a larger audience and establish yourself as an expert in your field. Each speaking opportunity led to more invitations, creating a snowball effect that significantly expanded my visibility.

Media coverage also played a crucial role. Journalists and bloggers often look for experts to interview or quote, and being a published author makes you an attractive candidate. I reached out to media outlets, offering my expertise on topics related to my book. This not only brought attention to my book but also to my business, attracting new clients and partnerships.

Building long-term relationships with readers and clients became easier, too. Readers who connected with my book often reached out for advice, consultation, or further services. These initial interactions were based on the trust and credibility established through my book. I made it a point to engage with my readers, responding to their questions and feedback, which helped build a loyal community around my brand.

In many ways, the book acted as a catalyst, sparking growth and creating new opportunities for my business. It wasn't just about the immediate sales but about the ongoing impact. Every new reader was a potential client, collaborator, or advocate. By leveraging my book effectively, I was able to transform my business, expanding its reach and solidifying its place in the market.

The journey from writing to leveraging a book for business growth is one of the most rewarding experiences I've had. It taught me the power of sharing knowledge and the importance of establishing authority in your field. If you're considering writing a book, know that its potential extends far beyond the pages. It's a tool that can propel your business to new levels of success, opening doors and creating opportunities you might never have imagined.

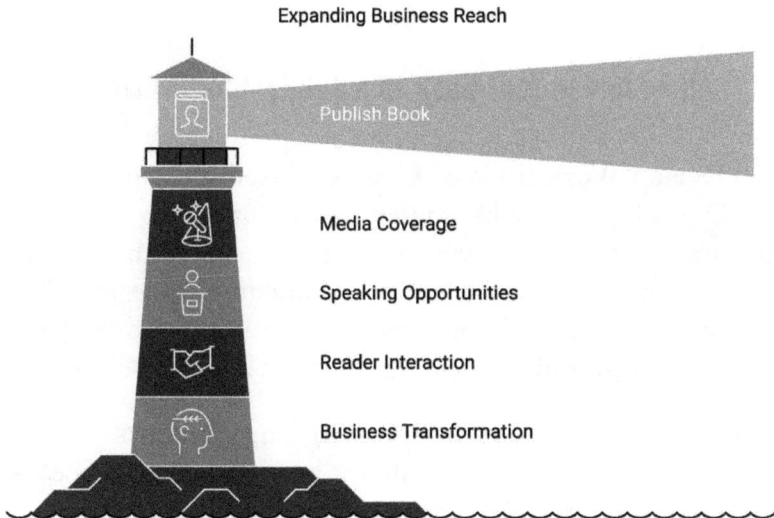

I worked with Amanda, who wanted to use her book to grow her consulting business. When we started, she didn't fully realize the potential her book had as a catalyst for growth. I guided her through positioning the book as a key part of her brand. Once published, Amanda's book quickly became her business card. Readers began reaching out to her for consultations, having already developed a sense of trust from the book's content.

Soon after, Amanda was invited to speak at industry events, where she connected with potential clients and partners. By leveraging her book strategically, she saw an increase in both speaking opportunities and client inquiries. The book acted as a credibility booster, making her a go-to expert in her field. This led to a steady stream of new clients, media appearances, and speaking engagements—all of which expanded her business far beyond what she had initially expected. The book became the catalyst that transformed her business into a more visible and reputable brand.

How to Use Your Book as a Catalyst for Growth

1. Develop Workshops or Courses Based on Your Book

Expand your book's content into workshops or online courses. For instance, if your book is about leadership, create a course that dives deeper into team-building strategies. This not only provides additional revenue but also reinforces your authority in your niche, helping you reach a broader audience.

2. Promote Your Book in Speaking Engagements

Use your book as a credibility booster to secure speaking opportunities. Highlight your book's success or unique insights when pitching yourself. For example, mention key lessons from the book that align with the audience's interests. Speaking engagements let you connect directly with potential clients and promote your book at the same time.

3. Offer Consulting or Coaching Services

Position your book as a stepping stone to higher-value services like consulting or coaching. For instance, if your book focuses on marketing strategies, offer one-on-one coaching to help clients implement those ideas. This approach turns readers into clients and creates a deeper impact through personalized support.

4. Expand Your Book into a Series

If your book is successful, consider writing follow-ups or a series to keep readers engaged. For example, a productivity book could lead to sequels on goal-setting or habit formation. A series keeps your audience invested in your content and allows you to build a comprehensive body of work.

5. Maintain Relationships with Readers

Stay connected with your audience through newsletters, webinars, or exclusive online communities. For instance, host live Q&A sessions where readers can ask questions about the book. Ongoing engagement keeps your book relevant and fosters long-term loyalty, ensuring your readers continue to value your expertise.

Conclusion

Recap of *The Book Wealth System*

As we wrap up this journey, let's take a moment to reflect on the key points we've covered in *The Book Wealth System*. We began with Book Writing 2.0, where we discussed the importance of understanding your audience and crafting a compelling narrative. We explored how to write with clarity and authority, ensuring your message is both powerful and accessible. We tackled writer's block and learned techniques to maintain momentum and productivity.

Next, in Book Publishing 2.0, we delved into the modern publishing landscape, weighing the pros and cons of self-publishing versus traditional publishing. We also looked at how to prepare your manuscript, from professional editing to formatting for different platforms, and we learned about the crucial role of a professional book cover in capturing readers' attention.

Finally, in Book Launch 2.0, we covered the steps to a successful book launch. We discussed the importance of creating a detailed launch plan, executing effective promotional strategies, and maintaining post-launch engagement to keep the momentum going. We also explored how to use your book as a tool for lead generation and business growth.

The Book Wealth System Roadmap

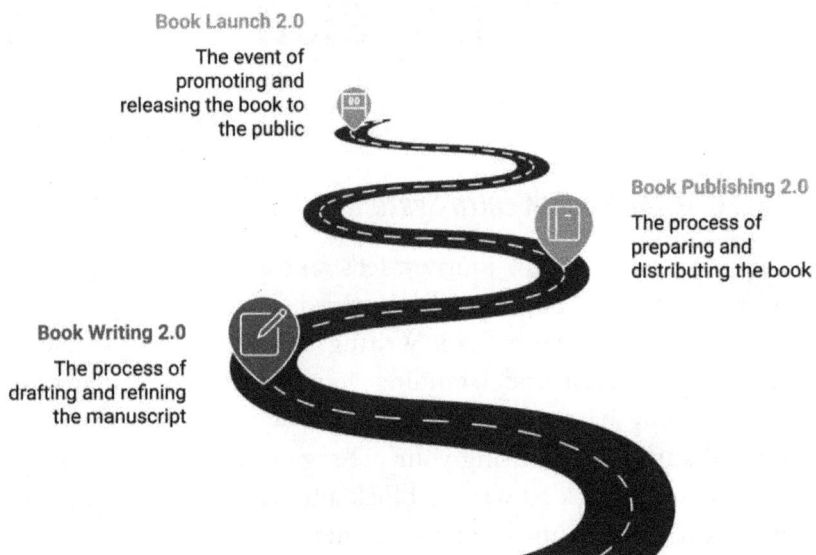

Book Launch 2.0

The event of
promoting and
releasing the book to
the public

Book Publishing 2.0

The process of
preparing and
distributing the book

Book Writing 2.0

The process of
drafting and refining
the manuscript

What to Do Next

If you read this whole book (about an hour's worth of reading), you have enough information to write a book that creates massive authority *and* generates tons of leads for your business.

Start by planning and writing a book that your ideal readers and clients actually want. This is the first step we take when people pay us to run the Book Wealth System for them. We take a deep dive into their ideal client profile to discover what their biggest pains and struggles are and how to provide the exact solution they want the most.

To get started, I suggest answering these three questions first:

1. Who is your ideal client?
2. What are their big struggles that you solve?
3. How do you solve those struggles?

The more in-depth you answer those, the better they'll serve you. Understanding the answers to those questions at a deep level will help you write a book that grabs your ideal clients' interest and keeps them engaged and wanting more.

If you want to explore how the Book Wealth System can replace all of your other marketing efforts and take your business to $1MM and beyond, just email me at chris@jetlaunch.net.

THIS BOOK IS PROTECTED INTELLECTUAL PROPERTY

Instant IP™

The author of this book values Intellectual Property. The book you just read is protected by Instant IP™, a proprietary process, which integrates blockchain technology giving Intellectual Property "Global Protection." By creating a "Time-Stamped" smart contract that can never be tampered with or changed, we establish "First Use" that tracks back to the author.

Instant IP™ functions much like a Pre-Patent™ since it provides an immutable "First Use" of the Intellectual Property. This is achieved through our proprietary process of leveraging blockchain technology and smart contracts. As a result, proving "First Use" is simple through a global and verifiable smart contract. By protecting intellectual property with blockchain technology and smart contracts, we establish a "First to File" event.

Protected by Instant IP™

LEARN MORE AT INSTANTIP.TODAY